Pr:
Trauma-Infor

MW01032104

"I was gripped by the prologue to this book and could hardly put it down as each chapter unpacked the what, why, and how of trauma-informed pastoral care. And the book's subtitle is so timely: *How to Respond When Things Fall Apart*. It fits our society's current reality—managing the Covid-19 pandemic, reckoning with racial trauma, and dealing with political polarization and many other traumas church leaders and those we serve are experiencing. But as Karen McClintock points out, our faith uniquely equips us to address these challenges if we learn how to recognize and respond to trauma, whether personal, generational, or secondary. This book both inspires and equips clergy and other congregational leaders and servants to become trauma informed."

—R. Lawson Bryan, resident bishop, South Georgia Area,
The United Methodist Church

"McClintock's work illustrates the importance of understanding trauma in a world deeply wounded by living through pandemics, natural disasters, systemic injustices, and interpersonal trauma. Her experiences ground her work as she provides insight into trauma theory and recovery, while also offering strategies for clergy, first responders, and others involved in pastoral and spiritual care. McClintock is not afraid to tackle challenging issues as she offers possibility and the hope of thriving for those who know trauma and for those who care for self and others."

—Joretta Marshall, emerita professor of pastoral theology
and care, Brite Divinity School, and coauthor of
Practicing Care in Rural Congregations and Communities

"In *Trauma-Informed Pastoral Care: How to Respond When Things Fall Apart*, Karen McClintock offers an in-depth look through the lens of trauma at current events, including the Covid-19 pandemic, natural disasters, racism, and sexual abuse. She reminds us that experienced trauma is about what happens inside us as a result of what happens to us. Certainly in the church, we have an obligation to offer healing. We also have much to learn as a society to become trauma informed and to always reflect compassion in our response. This is essential reading for anyone interested in understanding the impact of trauma in one's life."

—Becky Posey Williams, senior director for sexual ethics and advocacy, General Commission on the Status and Role of Women, The United Methodist Church

Trauma-Informed Pastoral Care

Trauma-Informed Pastoral Care

How to Respond When Things Fall Apart

KAREN A. McCLINTOCK

Fortress Press
Minneapolis

CONTENTS

PROLOGUE

Moonlight streamed through the glass doors, elongating my shadow on the carpeted living room floor where I sat. I watched the moon dip down behind silhouetted mountains. I'd draped my daughter's Winnie-the-Pooh afghan around my shoulders and cradled my knees, which were shaking despite my arms being around them. In this upright fetal position, I rocked and breathed more deeply with each motion. In breath, rock back. Outbreath, rock forward. After the shaking subsided, I released sighs and tears I'd suppressed for hours.

Instinctively, I began singing, although I don't recall which song. I have a "go-to" collection of comforting songs in my head, and since I have been a sign language interpreter at church, I have memorized more than one hymnal's worth of lyrics. In the darkness on my living room floor, I needed a calming and reassuring song. Perhaps it was the one that went "Don't be afraid. My love is stronger, my love is stronger than your fear . . ." from the Iona Community in Scotland. I breathe more slowly and deeply whenever I sing it. Even now as I write about this experience and hum the tune, lingering trauma lets go again, reminding me that, without volition, I have carried this night in my body for a very long time.

I was exhausted, coming home off the night shift as the on-call chaplain at a regional medical center where I worked while I completed my doctoral studies in psychology. The previous evening, my pager had gone off as I finished my supper at home. I changed clothes quickly, got into my car, and drove not far behind an ambulance headed in the same direction. I didn't know it at the time, but the ambulance was transporting a slight, blond, six-year-old boy who minutes before had been struck down by a car while crossing the street near his home. The driver hadn't seen him run out into the street, and—blessedly, I could say (but might not)—it was over fast.

By the time I'd parked behind the ambulance and entered the emergency room, his parents knew for certain that he could not be saved. I introduced myself to them, and we were ushered into an unadorned, nine-by-ten-foot windowless room with one hospital bed and a bench along the opposite wall. While the boy's father paced the halls, his mother climbed up onto the bed and cradled her son in her arms. She touched him so very gently. I stood in the doorway, resisting a scene I didn't want to move closer to. I pushed back fears about the unimaginable sudden loss of my daughter, letting this inevitable transference wash through me. After I shivered. The boy's mother said she wanted me to stay with them, so I sat down on the bench. Every fiber in my body wanted to run, knowing that I could catch this trauma and that I inevitably would catch it. We were in the room for hours.

I listened when she occasionally spoke. I silently prayed when she cried. I was not there to intercede, to interview, or to preach. It was my job to witness.

I had another job that night—keeping the coroner at a distance. He'd come to "retrieve the body," he told me in the hall. He didn't have all night, he added, placing his hands on his hips for emphasis. His face became red and angry, instinctively designed to intimidate me.

I want to point out here that I am a small female, acculturated to be kind and polite and to do what males in authority tell me to do. But not this time. I channeled the subpersonality my writing friends call "she who will not be moved."

"You can go and come back, or you can wait, but we are not telling that mother that she has to give up her sweet baby boy until she is ready!"

I think now, in writing this, about the way elephants grieve their dead family members, about people whose dead loved ones are laid out in the family parlor for visitors to come see, and about how people speak quietly and respectfully around the deceased. In other cultures, there wouldn't be a coroner knocking on the door, cruelly hastening the separation of the living from the dead.

An hour or two later, a nurse cracked open the door to our tomb and said the coroner was still in the waiting area, fuming. And I went out to him again and repeated my she-bear speech about how he wasn't getting the body anytime soon—or maybe soon, but it was the mother's decision. The nurse thanked me. Maybe I'd been silently singing my "go-to" hymn about standing on the rock of my savior. I didn't feel personally strong; I was only acting on instinct, like the elephant family. Just sit. Just sit there and embody the compassion within God's grieving heart.

I never asked or knew anything about the mother's beliefs, her church background, or how she would mend her soul after this trauma. Around 3:00 a.m., she released the boy and stood beside his bed, caressing his face and neatly folding the sheet around him. She looked over at me and said she would like a few minutes alone, and I stepped into the hall. In a short while, she cracked open the door and asked me to send in her husband. They said goodbye to their son in a room without candles or stained glass, a cold barren space nearly as dark as the morgue. About twenty minutes later, they emerged, heads down, and took a seat in an impersonal lobby to talk to a nurse about the next steps and to sign some necessary papers.

The staff, I learned, had all been trauma debriefed hours before by a psychologist I knew from the community. He had gathered them around a small lunch table and asked them to talk about their feelings and responses to the child's death. There were boxes of tissues on the table—largely still unopened.

Learning about the meeting, I was miffed. I thought, "Great, I've been the one in the room with the trauma and grief, and the debriefing was over hours ago. Who is going to debrief me?" The therapist had gone home, and the staff had moved on to other crises. (Much later during my career as a psychologist, I would learn that this type of immediate debriefing can do more harm than good, but no one knew that at the time.) I felt abandoned and alone. I walked numbly to my car and headed home.

I didn't get far into my house before I ended up rocking, crying, and singing on my living room floor. I looked out those sliding glass doors, desperate to see evidence that the sun would come up as always. Nearly an hour later, I called my sweet sister, a nurse who lived in Ohio at the time. The three-hour time difference meant she was awake, dressed, and ready for her commute to work. After she answered, I felt a little stupid for calling; I was not ready to tell much of the story.

I needed what Piglet needed from Pooh: "I just wanted to be sure of you"—loving, reliable attachment. I asked her to pray for me and for the family throughout the day. It was a short call because she had to hit the road. Most people were blithely beginning a normal day. I sat unmoving long after she said goodbye, until my shadow faded as the eastern sunrise finally threw golden light across the hills.

CHAPTER ONE

THE GROWING NEED FOR TRAUMA CARE

Gracious and loving Spirit, we give you thanks for this time apart to read and reflect. We depend on your presence. We turn to you for your steady and constant love in the midst of so much pain in our souls, our communities, our nation, and our world. Grant us full awareness of your wide embracing love as we turn our thoughts to victims of trauma and to our own experiences of traumatic injury and pain. Give us insight and courage. Equip us to better serve those who have been traumatized as we dedicate this time to them.

I am writing this book, and you are likely reading it, in the most trauma-inducing years of our adult lives—years that include millions of worldwide deaths and lockdowns due to the pandemic; job losses; food insecurity and houselessness on massive scales; exposed racial injustices; political and social unrest. Catastrophic wildfires are consuming farms, homes, and wildernesses; ice storms, tornadoes, and hurricanes are becoming more destructive, and more frequent. I know that many of these traumatic experiences are causing pain and grief for you and the members of your faith community.

In this book, you will read about people with different types of trauma, including some who carry unique traumatic burdens. You will become familiar with trauma's initial and long-lasting mental and physical symptomology. You will learn to recognize and heal lingering traumatic shadows from the pandemic. You will inevitably explore your own trauma, from the recent past to as far back as your immigrant or Indigenous ancestors. And then you will learn ways to heal trauma and build trauma resilience. Each chapter is designed to help you serve others by bringing trauma awareness to all aspects of your pastoral care.

WHAT IS TRAUMA?

Let's begin by exploring trauma's two main components. Trauma can be the result of circumstances outside of our control—things that happen to us—like a car crash, a physical assault, earthquakes, a pandemic, and such. These life-disrupting, painful experiences shake us to the core and cause us to rethink goals, relationships, core beliefs, and faith. This is the first component.

But trauma also has a second component—what happens inside our bodies during those experiences, the way our central nervous system fires up so we can escape pain or death and live to talk about it another day. Life-threatening experiences activate and forever change our brains' prefrontal cortex (the area that manages impulse control, story formation, and executive functioning) along with our bodies' inner processing centers that energize us during fear and calm us down thereafter.

Trauma expert Bessel Van Der Kolk's classic book is aptly named *The Body Keeps the Score*. Trauma is initially an external experience with an internal response, but without therapeutic intervention—and even sometimes with it—trauma lingers in our bodies. Trauma then becomes an internal experience with an external response.

The *Diagnostic and Statistical Manual of Psychiatric Disorders* (*DSM-5*) avoids any single definition of the word *trauma* and instead identifies symptom clusters that appear after a traumatic single event or multiple events. When those symptoms persist, causing mentally and physically uncomfortable reactions, they are fit into categories called disorders, which we will take a look at in the next chapter. Trauma is defined by what takes place inside us when we become alarmed and afraid, but it can also be identified in the physical and emotional scars it leaves behind.

BECOMING FAMILIAR WITH TRAUMA

For the next few pages, I invite you to notice the different types of trauma I describe. See if you can identify the trauma symptoms I illustrate and the trauma-relieving strategies I include in each story.

A few years ago, my husband and I bought our first SUV to expand our horizons with a road trip. We went to Arizona in December to visit family and then on to Los Angeles to spend Christmas Day with friends. The next morning, we had planned to head home to Oregon, but the I-5 freeway, called "the Grapevine," was packed with snow, ice, and stranded vehicles and was not expected to be clear for several days. We had time on our hands, so we took the scenic drive, not realizing that everyone else heading north would take it too.

We drove in stop-and-go traffic for six hours from LA to Santa Barbara, stopped for a meal, and since hotels were all full, decided to push farther north. As the traffic cleared about an hour later, drivers were like caged animals whose gates had been thrown open. On a curvy divided four-lane highway, the traffic thinned out and sped up. Then it suddenly stopped. A person two cars ahead of us made an overly fast lane change, forcing everyone to brake. We heard screeching tires and a crash. My husband tried frantically to avoid the car ahead by pumping the brakes and steering us toward the uncertain terrain of the center island, but we still crashed into the car ahead.

Thoughts flashed through my mind so fast I couldn't tell you what they were. Next thing I knew, we were checking in with each other. "Are you okay?" "Yes. Are you?" "Yes, I think so." The inside cabin was remarkably intact, and as my husband got out to check on the woman in front of us, the OnStar lady provided some relief: "It appears you've been in a crash; do you need an ambulance?" "No," I said, sighing deeply, letting my shaking body ease up a bit. "Where are you?" she asked. I hadn't a clue. Now, this is a GPS system, right? "Maybe you can tell me," I said. The irony helped me laugh away more tension.

A saintly highway patrol officer found us a hotel, and the next day we left the car in San Luis Obispo for three months of major repairs. A rental car and clearer roads took us home to rebalance our equilibrium by reconnecting with friends and family. In the first few weeks, I told the story a dozen times or more, each time reliving and releasing it.

What's Going on Here?

A car crash is a good example of a singular traumatic experience—a life-threatening moment over which one has no control. Eighty percent of the time, people who experience this type of uncomplicated, short-lived trauma do not go on to develop a diagnosable mental illness. Most recover fully.

During and immediately after the crash, I never lost consciousness, I didn't witness my husband or anyone being seriously injured, and I soon knew that everything was all right. After the crash, I slept well, and my memories about that day were easily and comfortably retrieved. Did this trauma linger? Yes, on rare occasions when road conditions deteriorate and I consider driving, my pulse goes up and my hands get clammy—a few physical remnants. It would be a chicken-and-egg debate to explore whether my memories of the crash lead to these physical symptoms or I have unconscious physical symptoms that arise and prompt me to think, "It's dangerous out there; maybe I shouldn't go." The good news is that I can sort out those old anxieties. I have learned to reduce and release them in order to get in the car for another trip.

Relax and Breathe

Reading this section, you may have noticed tension in your body, especially if you have experienced a frightening car accident. Before going on, take a minute to breathe deeply, stand up and walk around the room, scan your environment through your senses (touch, sound, smell, sight, taste). These mindfulness techniques can ground you in the present moment and will help you focus on the reading. Give yourself permission to take a longer break if you need to shake off and release old memories or awakened physical symptoms.

EXPLORING TRAUMA IN THE PANDEMIC

While I write this book, the Covid-19 pandemic is still raging around the world, but US deaths have slowed as vaccinations have become widely available. The pandemic has caused millions of deaths, and studies about the trauma legacy it leaves behind will be forthcoming. Unlike the trauma from a single incident, Covid-19 trauma has consumed several years and has been full of multiple traumatic moments and prolonged stressors.

Covid-19 brought contagion fear, disrupted routines, tragic losses, and disconnection from typical sources of comfort—our family and friends. With little data to go on and misinformation rampant, our basic belief that we could protect ourselves from harm disappeared. For the foreseeable future, many people will still be grieving. People who carried multiple traumas with them into the pandemic felt even greater triggered physical and mental anguish. Safety and connection, trauma's healing opposites, were just not consistently available.

So many lives were disrupted by the pandemic that as we come out of it, we need to create safety nets for basic welfare such as jobs, housing, health care, and mental health treatment. Psychologist Abraham Maslow developed a well-known theory in the late 1940s that suggested a hierarchy of human needs. He proposed that psychological and spiritual well-being can be tended to only after our basic physical needs (health, shelter, and food, for example) are taken care of. Jesus worked from a similar hierarchy in service to others. He healed the sick, visited the incarcerated, fed the hungry, and then tended to their broken hearts. It's good spiritual care and good trauma-informed care.

Pandemic Trauma

Early in the pandemic, along with many others, I became addicted to "doomscrolling" (the tendency to track anxiety-producing "bad" news by reading newspapers online and scrolling through social media sites). Psychologists who study people's attitudes about misery have discovered that the adage "misery loves company" is true only if the company is miserable too. In other words, misery loves *miserable* company. Doomscrolling seemed helpful at first—distraction can lower anxiety—but it also leads to unproductive avoidance. It is actually a trauma response that psychologists call hypervigilance. When we don't feel safe, we scan the environment for enemies, so we'll be ready to run or hide if we need to. In Covid-19 we had nowhere to run, so we read and watched and listened to more news.

The *New York Times* online, my primary source, offered me a smorgasbord of misery, posting charts with Covid-19 case numbers from around the world as US deaths climbed unimaginably higher, tapered off, and surged again. Pictures and interviews told stories about racial discrimination and social inequity. Many of us read and cried and railed against false narratives, flawed vaccine distribution, a conflicted congress, and delayed or confounding national and local responses. Numerous personal losses and reports from chaplains, doctors, and nurses on the front lines broke our hearts.

Coping Strategies

To get me out of the house safely in the pandemic's first months, my husband bought a map of our southwestern Oregon college town with the goal to walk every street. We spent lockdowns walking and talking to relieve our misery, and afterward highlighting those streets on the map. Passing through the downtown area provided us with a reality check on Covid-19's economic devastation—businesses were closed, signs on every door described safety protocols, and restaurants posted new "food to go" menus.

Walking through the railroad district was like taking a pilgrimage or prayer walk. People had hung Black Lives Matter flags and memorial T-shirts on the chain link fence, naming innocent people killed by police—Breonna Taylor, Stephon Clark, Botham Jean, and Aura Rosser. The name George Floyd would soon be added. By year's end, nearly our whole city map was highlighted. But while the walking helped, we didn't walk off our grief or all of our stress.

Cortisol relentlessly pumped through our bodies. Would we make it through the pandemic alive, or would we die alone, gasping for air on a respirator at the hospital? Nature appeared to be random, but I was less physically vulnerable than my husband, so I took on the task of protecting us both by going out infrequently. I paid local businesses over the phone and asked clerks to leave my purchases in bags on the sidewalk. I said, "Sorry, I don't share air" and frequently told my husband to order it (whatever *it* was) online because it was "not worth dying for." We experienced feelings our non-White neighbors have felt on a daily basis throughout their lives—substantially unsafe every day.[1]

We distracted ourselves as often as possible, had our first gin and tonics in years (one each), and ordered the Disney Channel. These strategies helped, but they couldn't wipe out the trauma load. The traumatized body seeks reassurance, but we weren't comforted by our "normal" connections. We reached out to our single friends who felt this loneliness even more acutely. We were reminded with every text, email, and video call that loved ones and dear ones were getting sick, suffering ongoing symptoms, and dying. Grieving our nation's health care abuse legacy, we felt ashamed and outraged that Black, Brown, Indigenous, and other marginalized communities were grossly discriminated against throughout the pandemic—in the availability of hospital beds, respirators, treatments, and vaccines—and died at exponentially higher rates than White people in the United States.

Pandemic Denial

Depending on where any of us lived at the time, our political affiliation, our ethnicity, and our religious affiliation, we may have approached the Covid-19 threat differently. A large swath of the American public and people on social media platforms decried the pandemic as "fake news." Denial and minimization are protective functions people use to avoid pain. Denial that Covid-19 was anything worse than a flu was a defense mechanism many people used to repress fear. No small number of people refused to admit or recognize that something life-threatening was occurring. A woman who lived in a community where the pandemic was often scoffed at as "overblown" and "exaggerated" told a friend that her grandmother had died in a board-and-care facility. Her companion asked, "Did she have Covid?" The woman replied, "Well, she had Covid, but she didn't die of it."

For many people, traumatic components of Covid-19 led to social withdrawal and deteriorating mental health (i.e., increased suicidality, addiction, and anxiety). Domestic violence and child abuse were underreported while increasing exponentially. Other people fought against social isolation by taking risks and became sick after attending social gatherings, funerals, or worship. When voluntary vaccinations lagged, and the Delta variant spread, family members and faith communities became politically divided.

Fear was understandably prevalent among vulnerable populations. American Indians and Alaska Natives, Black people, and Latinx people who caught the virus were far more likely to be seriously ill and hospitalized than non-Hispanic Whites and were more than twice as likely to die.[2] At the start of the pandemic, a high percentage of all Covid-19 deaths occurred in senior care facilities, severing the bonds between beloved elders and their families forever. People who developed serious neurological disabilities and other conditions known as "long haul" symptoms told their stories to the press in order to combat those who claimed that the virus was no worse than an ordinary flu. These people could not ignore or deny their overwhelming losses or their pain.

While chaplains and clergy on the front lines helped people die with dignity and grieved family members' deaths, many of them resided in communities where Covid-19 was minimized or denied, worsening their trauma. I liken this to a young woman who goes home at the holidays and finds the courage to tell her family that as a preteen she was molested by a family member, only to be told that she was "making it all up." At that point she experiences retraumatization.

Retraumatization

Retraumatization is a physical or emotional reaction to a situation, interpersonal encounter, or current event that replicates an original trauma. Responses to current stimuli are intensified by one or more previous traumatic experiences. For example, when a victim's story (pain, abuse, trauma) is denied, this re-creates the lack of control and powerlessness that occurred during the victim's initial trauma.

Many people were retraumatized during the pandemic. When a nurse got off her shift late one night and went to the grocery store, she saw a person in line behind her without a mask and, seeing a stack of them nearby, offered to buy the mask for him and asked him to put it on. He scoffed at her and said, "I would wear one if I needed to." She had watched a man his age die just hours before. She was retraumatized and didn't feel safe. She left the store without her food and went home in tears. Similar moments disheartened healthcare workers trying to save unvaccinated patients in intensive care units months after vaccinations had become widely available.

Although people have responded to the pandemic in a variety of ways, psychologists can say that for the first time since the 1918 Spanish flu, millions of people around the world simultaneously experienced trauma. Even people who denied or underplayed the seriousness of the pandemic had their lives disrupted by it. Some of them responded with anger, aimed at victims, politicians, and medical workers because they didn't know how to blame a virus for their psychological anxiety. Everyone responded with fear, whether they named it or sublimated it. When I told people I was writing a book on trauma during the pandemic, people asked, "Where do you start?" or said, "That'll be a long book!"

What's Going on Here?

Trauma is an experience that overwhelms normal coping mechanisms. To protect us during repeatedly stressful times, our bodies remain on high alert. They co-opt the executive functions in the frontal lobes of our brains. A new normal emerges as trauma slows down operational memory, interferes with retention, and makes it harder to multitask. Experts suggested that during the worst months of the pandemic, most of us started each day at about 30 percent arousal (in fight, flight, or freeze) due to our bodies' natural inclination to protect us. Our bodies instinctually responded to fear by shutting down the frontal lobes in our brains, including the rationalizing, planning, and organizing systems. Thus, the term "Covid fog" came into popular usage.

Bearing this anxiety load over many months of living with Covid-19, we did not grow more at ease. Being "stuck" together presented us with relational challenges. Locked at home together, couples got in each other's way, felt irritable about petty things. Families home schooling children were perhaps even literally "climbing the walls." The media coined yet another term, "Covid fatigue," aptly applied to the state of physical and mental exhaustion people felt during the pandemic's prolonged stress. Many people just ran out of bandwidth for going anywhere or hearing one more sound bite of sad or frightening news. This was another signal that the pandemic had created long-term trauma fatigue.

CLERGY IN THE PANDEMIC

As clergy, you personally faced many of the challenges I have described. You also cared for trauma victims and survivors. Was it emotionally exhausting? Were you disconnected from people and experiences that typically nurture you while you handled other people's grief? Who did you miss the most? Who died in your extended family? What was it like to face the pressure to speak prophetically about pandemic trauma and loss? Did you feel prepared for this role?

We all hope to never face a pandemic on this scale again. But the pandemic has provided new insights about trauma care on a massive scale. More work lies ahead as people heal their traumatic grief and as we work to correct the social injustices the pandemic laid bare. We now have an obligation and opportunity to become trauma healers in the days, weeks, and years ahead. It might be tempting to put these years of pandemic trauma into the past with relief and without examination or intentional repair. This would do a disservice to every person who died, every community unjustly impacted, and the nation at large.

The church has been and will always be a place of healing and renewal and the training ground for social justice movements. As with other traumatic experiences, we will not be the same hereafter. Business as usual has been exposed as inherently racist and classist. Underresourced people and millions of unemployed people need the church to step up at this time, not to retreat back into the safety that power and privilege offer. The only way forward from here is for clergy and congregations to become trauma-informed and to work for personal, community, and national healing.

How will we, as clergy who care, ease our own and others' lingering trauma? Those doomscrolled images will remain seared in our memories long after the pandemic is over. We will need rituals for remembrance, times when we safely let ourselves grapple with what just happened and talk about it. We will need to tell many stories and be heard many times. Now that we can worship "live" and in person again, we can even more effectively assist people in our communities who remain financially devastated, grief stricken, or otherwise devastated by this pandemic.

THE HEALING BEGINS

In the chapters ahead, I invite you to look through the trauma lens with me. I will introduce you to clergy who provide trauma care in diverse settings. By the end of the book, you will have learned to recognize trauma symptoms in yourself and others, along with ways to foster healing from trauma. You may be a pastor or rabbi serving a congregation, a hospital chaplain, or another faith leader with a commitment to serving others. You know the risks and rewards of these roles. You have likely cherished moments when someone trusted you enough to share their private wounds and said, "I've never told anyone this before. . . ." You have already witnessed tremendous pain and miraculous healing. But there is much more work to do, and this resource will help you deepen your understanding of the trauma within every individual you care for. It will help you assess the secondary trauma you have unwittingly "caught" by being with trauma victims. And it will lay out strategies to help you become more trauma resilient in your work.

Perhaps you took a psychology course in college. Your professor likely warned you to avoid self-diagnoses. As you read this book on trauma, you will inevitably recognize your own trauma history. You may want to keep a journal to help you identify any past or present traumas as they reveal themselves to you along the way. As you read through each chapter, pay close attention to physical sensations and feelings that arise and note them in the journal too. I have added exercises throughout the book to help you remain calm as you read stories or contents that could be triggering. If you feel increasingly unsettled in any way, set the book aside for a while or talk over the material with a spiritual director, trusted loved one, or therapist.

CHAPTER TWO

TRAUMA-INFORMED PASTORAL CARE

AN ADAPTED MODEL

Source of life, solid ground beneath our feet. The Psalms proclaim
your ever-present comfort. Where can we run from your love? If we
climb to heaven, you are there; when everything goes to hell, you
are there too! Even the darkness is as light to you. When we awaken
at dawn, you welcome us with opportunities for love and service.
Trusting this, we breathe in your spirit deeply, we exhale gratitude,
and we turn strong to meet the day.

—Psalm 139:7–12, adapted

Think with me for a moment about how complex trauma can be. Trauma can start with one life-threatening incident or be caused by repeated incidents. Trauma can arise from witnessing violence as well as being a victim of violence. When a current trauma intersects with past traumas, our bodies remember, relive, and reenact the old ones. Luckily, as clergy who care for and about others, it's not up to us to diagnose people or label them by their mental health conditions. But the more we learn about trauma's aftereffects, the better prepared we are to recognize and respond to trauma victims appropriately, by avoiding reinjury and facilitating healing. This is called trauma-informed care.

Trauma-informed care is a specific treatment approach in the mental health field. In the past two decades, social work programs, drug and alcohol treatment facilities, and mental health care clinics have been training their staff to recognize and treat trauma. We who are clergy regularly and instinctively respond to traumatic situations, but we often do so without specific training. As the old saying goes, we rely on a wing and a prayer. While we have wisdom and experience to build on, we have a lot to learn about trauma and trauma care.

Borrowing from the theory and guiding principles of trauma-informed care in other fields, we can learn to respond proactively rather than reactively during and after traumatic situations. While we are not technically first responders, a role that implies medical intervention, we *are* frequently first responders when it comes to mental and spiritual health. We help individuals, congregations, and communities by coming alongside people during highly stressful times and are often the first to receive a call in an emergency.

Due to their traumatic contents, I clearly recall the times in my local church ministry when I received desperate calls. A woman called me after she had gone to the garage and found her boyfriend dead by suicide. She had stumbled into her kitchen, grabbed the phone, and dialed 911. I was the next call. The evocative image she described has blessedly faded away for me. What I do clearly remember is the view out my window while I took the call.

I can also picture the wood paneling in another church office on the day when a social worker brought a preteen to my office, enlisting my help as she told the girl that her mother had died in a car crash that morning. I remember the parsonage kitchen where I took a mother's call from a specialty hospital to tell me her daughter had just died from a rare form of cancer. These are all situations in which I served as a first responder. It was my job to wait on the line until an ambulance came, to offer calm, logical support when trauma made it impossible for these people to think clearly, to help them plan their next steps. I offered emergency spiritual and mental health care.

During these past years of prolonged pandemic trauma, systemic racial violence laid bare, and natural disasters like floods and fires, you have probably responded with various levels of skill and experience in trauma care when reaching out to hurting people who have asked for your help. Since all trauma upends faith, you may have listened to a victim's uncertainties about God and anger within their grief. Many of you know intuitively and through training in pastoral care or clinical pastoral education how to advocate for others. While you may not have framed your ministry this way, you have already been providing trauma care. As you read ahead, you will learn a good deal more about effective care strategies and some pitfalls to avoid.

This book is designed to help you cherish the blessings in this first-responder role and be consciously competent. When you were called by God to your vocation, it wasn't a call to the role of EMT, and yet the times demand you play this role. How you respond in these circumstances can influence a trauma survivor's long-term recovery—for the worse if your care is delivered in a trauma-insensitive manner and for the better if you are trauma-informed.

THE "TRAUMA-INFORMED" CARE APPROACH

In 1994, the US Substance Abuse and Mental Health Services Administration (SAMHSA) began publishing information and guidelines for service organizations about a model for patient care that they called "trauma-informed." The term is now being used in most areas of public service and by mental health professionals. It indicates that every helping professional needs to understand trauma's toll on children, adults, and communities in their care. While different service agencies and mental health professionals define trauma care differently, the overall principles are similar across fields. These principles are designed to minimize client retraumatization and provider burnout through secondary trauma while enhancing trauma healing and building trauma resilience among the people served.

SAMHSA urged service providers to follow four guiding principles called the "Four Rs." As a person trained in ethics, I think these can be viewed as ethical principles. They weren't meant to establish specific services (i.e., treatments or outcomes) but rather to offer education about trauma symptoms and recovery in order to improve care. Faith communities and clergy may adopt these principles as well.

The Four Rs of Trauma-Informed Care

Realize trauma's impact on individuals and groups.

Recognize the signs and symptoms of trauma.

Respond to trauma with supportive services.

Resist retraumatization by creating safe, supportive, and collaborative partnerships with victims/survivors.[1]

Trauma-informed clergy learn ways to foster healing and ways to avoid harm. We are open-hearted and open-minded. We recognize physiological symptoms in people with mental health challenges or difficult personalities and get curious about what trauma lies beneath individual behaviors. We learn to step back while looking at people and avoid making judgments about them. We stay open to learning about each person's trauma legacy before jumping to ignorant conclusions. We affirm the wisdom in James Baldwin's observation: "People are trapped in history and history is trapped in them."[2]

Trauma-informed care is compassionate in the fullest sense of the word—grounded in our call to abide with suffering people. It is a way to serve individuals, congregations, and communities by understanding as much as possible about trauma and seeing people we are called to serve through a trauma lens. Everyone we work with, worship with, and reach out to has a trauma history, and some are currently symptomatic. We can become wise about the implications of their history and symptoms, particularly when generational trauma and injustice trauma are front and center. Once we grasp the underlying role trauma plays in most human interactions, we can educate staff, lay leaders, and congregants about best practices in trauma care.

Trauma-informed clergy serve their communities through collaborative partnerships with nonprofit and governmental agencies to assist people. We recognize that people of color (while not monolithic) are more likely than not to have a personal history of trauma and generational trauma. Trauma-informed clergy have studied the US history of violence and oppression causing Black-bodied trauma and racialized, White-bodied trauma. We familiarize ourselves with the traumatic residue carried by sexual abuse survivors, victims of domestic violence, immigrants, LGBTQ community members, and other groups who are frequently targeted, assaulted or killed, and denied justice. We recognize that for every traumatized person, friends, family members, and communities at large are also traumatized and that as congregations and communities overlap, they need one another because healing trauma takes the whole village.

Trauma-informed clergy have studied trauma's biological, psychological, social, and spiritual characteristics and use that knowledge to inform their ministry.

We have to take good care of ourselves in order to do this work, and a future chapter is dedicated to this topic. We can never fully avoid the spillover stress that trauma care potentiates, but we can learn stress inoculation techniques. By recognizing our own reactive states and learning to regulate our bodies' trauma response systems, we can become some of the calmest people in the room when strong emotions or violence erupts. Unconscious trauma arousal patterns lead us to avoidance behaviors, shame, or emotional disconnection when we are helping others, but conscious awareness can overcome these dynamics and help us remain level-headed, compassionate, and present.

While most clergy are not trained therapists, all of us have a uniquely important place in trauma care. We provide a specific healing modality known as pastoral care. We explore spiritual issues that arise in trauma, we speak about trauma in sermons and blogs, and we carry a faith-based belief that even after great pain, suffering, and loss, full recovery is possible. Once fully trained, we competently and confidently provide trauma-informed pastoral care. We do this work trusting that more often than not, even devastating traumatic events lead to healing and remarkable transformation.

TRAUMA-INFORMED CARE IN ACTION

Rear Admiral Chaplain Margaret Grun Kibben, a Presbyterian (USA) minister, began her work as chaplain to the US House of Representatives on Sunday, January 3, 2021. On the following Wednesday, January 6, she went to the US Capitol for a historic event—the confirmation of the national election. She entered the House chamber and soon after stood at a speaker's dais to deliver an invocation on what she knew was likely to be a contentious day. She bowed her head and read from Psalm 46, "God is our refuge and strength, a very present help in trouble." Her text foreshadowed the day.[3]

Angry protestors near the White House had gathered that morning and were watching President Donald Trump make his case that the election had been stolen. At his urging, they began marching toward the Capitol. They pushed past security barriers, climbed outer walls, and broke in through windows. Armed with assault rifles and wearing helmets and riot gear, they filled halls and passageways in the labyrinthine building. As their fear and anger escalated, they became violent. Chaplain Kibben heard them shouting and the chamber doors being thrashed and assaulted with makeshift weapons. The Capitol Police were outnumbered. Congress members and clerks stacked desks and chairs high against inside doors to the chamber but couldn't hold the intruders back for long.

Kibben was prepared for this moment. She had served in combat as the US Navy's chief chaplain. She'd offered prayers in war zones around the world, and she had learned to keep an inner calm, which she calls a "spiritual covering," even when she and others were threatened with death. As members of Congress ducked for cover, pulled out protective gas masks, and looked for ways to escape, a clerk asked her to pray again. Kibben had been silently praying all along, but she began to pray loudly to be heard over the melee.

A news reporter who huddled with others in the balcony that day said that she had kept her emotions in check until she saw people holding hands and kneeling in prayer. Kibben noted afterward, "It was a matter of asking for God's covering and a hedge of protection around us. . . . And that in the chaos, the spirit would descend in the room to offer us peace and order." Kibben didn't worry about her safety while being escorted to a location in the building's basement. She offered comfort to strangers around her. She was keenly focused on people she saw in the greatest distress. "There were people of varying abilities, health conditions and emotional states," she said. "My concern was to keep an eye on who was struggling, so that I could come alongside them."

She walked around the "safe" room, quietly speaking with staff, members of Congress, and Capitol Police. Describing her trauma-informed approach, she told news media that she reaches out to distressed people, "just taking them where they are and listening to what they're willing to share at that moment." She uses the term "come alongside" to describe her work, an apt phrase for trauma-informed responders. When she next offered prayer with them, she said that God too "[had] come alongside each and every one of [them]."[4]

Most clergy will not find themselves as Chaplain Kibben or Senate Chaplain Barry C. Black did on that day—among terrified people during an insurrection—but clergy are more and more frequently among the first to arrive moments after a traumatic experience. While trauma is by its very definition dangerous and unpredictable, trauma care skills make it possible to provide effective care. These skills can be learned and relied upon.

What Kibben Did That Was Trauma-Informed

Let me summarize Chaplain Kibben's trauma-informed care on that day during the violence at the Capitol. Kibben's ability to keep her focus when her body was on high alert was really quite remarkable. As she heard gunshots, shattering glass, and shouts resounding in the building's halls and chambers, she drew upon prayer's calming power and offered familiar words from Scripture. Through inclusive prayer, she reinforced the connection others had to their own anchoring beliefs. Her words literally changed the cortisol levels rushing through her body and the bodies around her.

Because of her training and experience as a military chaplain, Kibben recognized trauma symptoms in others. Perhaps the look on their faces told her of their terror; perhaps she saw them shaking or crying. Perhaps they were silent and staring off blankly. These would all be trauma responses. When safety was assured, she looked for those in greatest emotional peril from retriggered trauma and—not just intuitively, but through experience—used the faith within her soul to stay calm and trust in God. She listened to others without any expectations. By being in relationship to them, even as a perfect stranger, she helped them return to calmer emotional states.[5]

What Victims Experienced

In the aftermath of the Capitol takeover, we had a glimpse of how differently people describe their trauma. One senator said he wasn't afraid; he was just angry, not realizing that the arousal in his central nervous system was actually the same. People who were targeted by violence that day spoke about being traumatized, especially if they were trapped in offices or people of color targeted by hate groups. Representative Ayanna Pressley hid in her office that day and found that the emergency response call button had been ripped out. She was simultaneously trapped and terrorized. Senator Patty Murray's courageously honest interview with Judy Woodruff illustrated the toll intense fear can take during a lockdown situation.[6] She vividly recalled reaching out to text family members as her cell phone lost its charge, crawling across her office to search for gas masks, seeing the absurdity and heroism in her husband's leg pressed against the door to protect them, and hearing threatening voices in the hallway.

Every person in the melee that day had a different subjective experience. What they had in common was the biological response system that kicked in to help them evade attack by running to hiding places for safety. These trauma symptoms weren't new to some victims/ survivors that day, but they were to others.

What's Going on Here?
From our body's viewpoint, all trauma is physical. It starts with an event that triggers fight, flight, and freeze responses. Trauma operates

in our bodies before we can subjectively interpret what's happening. During frightening, life- or integrity-threatening events, fear races up our spinal cords, passes through complex vagal nerves, and activates our hindbrains. A complex system of brain signals helps us respond like all animals respond when threatened: we do whatever is necessary to survive. Some theorists believe that all trauma is physical. For example, in *My Grandmother's Hands*, therapist Resmaa Menakem writes, "Contrary to what many people believe, trauma is not primarily an emotional response. Trauma always happens in the body. It is a spontaneous protective mechanism used by the body to stop or thwart further (or future) potential damage."[7] The body that's overwhelmed is a traumatized body.

Physiological responses that are triggered by trauma can manifest days, months, or years later. People who lived through the invasion of the Capitol may discover lingering trauma symptoms. Capitol Police officers who tried to hold back violent rioters and people fleeing to safety both had activated central nervous systems.

Watching videos of the events certainly retraumatized them. Sometimes we learn about past traumatic material not by scanning our brains for memories but by noticing our body's reenactments (e.g., cold, sweaty hands; increased pulse; stomach growling; a higher tone of voice; or tremors).

On January 6, Chaplain Kibben's work at the Capitol had just begun because she will no doubt continue to help members of Congress understand and release their trauma. As clergy, we will all help recently traumatized victims in the weeks and years ahead. Learning and using trauma-informed perspectives and principles will ground our work and help individuals, congregations, and communities heal. We follow the SAMHSA four R's—realizing trauma's impact, recognizing its signs and symptoms, responding with support and supportive services, and resisting any biases or judgments that would add to the victim's pain through retraumatization.

A New "R" in Trauma-Informed Clergy Care

When Chaplain Kibben was with trauma victims at the Capitol, she described her work *relationally*. She came alongside victims, offered powerful prayers, and quoted Scripture. That's what clergy are trained to do, right? But you may not know that these common "tricks of the trade" have a lot in common with well-documented techniques to calm aroused central nervous systems. By reading Scripture and offering prayer, she mitigated against adrenal overloads and exhaustion, and then she connected her hearers to their belief in a holy, loving, protective presence. She reminded them that they weren't alone.

The Four Rs of trauma-informed care were developed by a governmental agency, and they are practical and useful. But as spiritual care providers, we need to add a fifth R to the list—reconnect. Reconnect victims to loved ones, caring communities, and faith.

Trauma is a relational wound involving broken trust, shattered attachment bonds, and spiritual upheaval. Trauma disconnects us from loved ones, dear ones, social support, and God. The good news? Clergy provide relational bridges. Building trauma resilience and trauma healing begins by connecting victims to social services, mental health providers, survivor support groups, and congregations. When a victim experiences God's abandonment, a spiritual director helps to restore the broken spiritual bond.

We can best help survivors by providing safety, choice, collaboration, trustworthiness, and empowerment. It's up to us to be sure that our care receivers feel safe and give them the lead role in their decision-making. We empower them and collaborate with them to foster growth and increase resiliency. We know that trust is a precious element in any caring relationship, and we build trust slowly. As they recover, we have the blessed opportunity to see miracles in the making.

CHAPTER THREE
WHAT HAPPENS DURING AND AFTER TRAUMA

Healing Spirit, come along with us as we learn more about trauma. We have seen you in the life Jesus lived. He touched rejected lepers, revived a sick child as her awestruck father watched and wept. He healed a woman bent over in sorrow and paid loving attention to people who had been pushed aside by callous onlookers. Equip us to embody him as we offer prayer or hold people who have collapsed in sobs and say, "I'm so, so, sorry."

THE DEVELOPMENT OF THE TRAUMA DIAGNOSIS

When did trauma first become a focus in mental health care? In America, psychiatrists explored trauma when they were working for the US military during and after the First World War. Thousands of soldiers returned home from battlefronts with lasting psychological injuries medical doctors could not treat or cure. Subsequently, the military tested new recruits to determine who could "pass the muster" and stay on the front lines under fire without breaking down emotionally or deserting. Who among them could be repeatedly redeployed, even after barely escaping battles wherein they watched as their fellow soldiers were maimed or killed?

The predictability rate in the tests they developed was not very high. Sure, a new recruit could sit down and fill out a questionnaire about an imaginary war situation (unlike any other situation they had ever encountered) and tell the military they'd be fit for duty. With strong loyalties to the nation and war effort, most were motivated to provide a good first impression by projecting invulnerability and strength. When they were on the battlefield, however, a soldier's "metal," as they called it, was unpredictable.

COMBAT FATIGUE

During and after World War II, when even more soldiers returned home with what was then called "combat fatigue" or "combat neurosis," my father became a treatment provider in a veterans' facility for shell-shocked soldiers. He was a psychologist fresh out of graduate school and an army veteran who felt guilty that he hadn't qualified for combat duty because of poor eyesight.

He began his work at the facility feeling proud to do more for the war effort. He sat next to soldiers in rows of beds and spoke to them softly as they stared blankly at the ceiling in total dissociation. He listened as others told their gruesome stories about what happened on the front. Daily, he heard them crying out in unbearable physical and psychological pain.

The medical community didn't have effective ways to manage the symptoms these soldiers brought home. Treatments were sometimes barbaric, like electroshock therapy and medications with excruciating side effects. Futility and hopelessness surrounded them. My father was expected to write a note about the patients' progress on the clipboard at the foot of the soldier's bed every day. He often despairingly wrote, "None."

What's Going on Here?

My father was thrown into trauma care long before anyone understood secondary trauma. He went to veterans' bedsides with not much more than his church-birthed compassion for them. He didn't have a supervisor to help him with what he was experiencing or to identify his emerging trauma symptoms.

Constantly witnessing and absorbing soldiers' anguish, he did not fare well. He wrote in a journal every day and plodded through what my mother later called "his darkest year." He became depressed and suicidal. The work did not assuage his guilt; it only multiplied it. He absorbed their trauma in deeply unconscious places–within images that showed up in nightmares. In dreams his body felt the bullets and the shrapnel, and he heard exploding bombs. He lost weight, he smoked a few more packs every day, and he paced the house at night.

Through the soldiers' stories about their trauma, trauma also lodged inside him. This was the only time my father–a young, closeted gay soldier in a straight life all of his sixty-four years–wrote about suicidal thoughts and feelings. My parents never told me how he ended his work with wounded veterans. But I know that he entirely gave up his hoped-for career as a psychologist and never again spoke about the veterans' hospital. His jobs thereafter were administrative, lived out within the protected walls of a university registrar's office.[1]

Secondary Trauma

Secondary trauma (also called "tertiary" trauma) is a term used to describe indirect exposure to trauma through a firsthand story or account of traumatic events. Stress from hearing repeated traumatic details can lead to symptoms similar to the primary victim's symptoms, including depression, anxiety, and spiritual malaise. After prolonged exposure, burnout is common.

EVOLVING PERSPECTIVES ON TRAUMA

With each subsequent war following World War II, solders stayed in battle for more extended tours of duty and were repeatedly returned to war zones. They were exposed to civilian deaths and the deaths of fellow soldiers more often, making their return home with trauma inevitable. Psychiatric researchers and therapists who worked with Korean War and Vietnam War veterans learned more about combat trauma and established protocols for trauma treatment. Common symptom clusters were identified and placed in diagnostic categories, but posttraumatic stress disorder (PTSD) was not added to psychiatric nomenclature until 1980.

In the decade before that, women who had previously been denied access to research labs, academic degrees, and peer-reviewed journals broke through barriers in education and became researchers and clinicians in the field of psychiatry. Women clearly looked at traumatic stress from a different viewpoint. Female providers began identifying sexual abuse trauma and documenting common symptoms.

The feminist movement brought sexual abuse and rape into public awareness. Minimization, victim blaming, and secret keeping about sexual abuse were common in psychiatry even at its inception. Sigmund Freud, often called the father of psychiatry, who began his early work as a physician in Vienna, studied dissociative symptoms in female patients. He posited that their symptoms had been caused by familial sexual abuse trauma, which was prevalent and extremely harmful. This conclusion did not sit well with his upper-class Austrian peer reviewers and the men who financially backed his research and laboratory. Under threat of losing his standing and funding, he basically had to come up with a new theory and switch the blame to his patients. He recanted much of his early work and developed a theory that his patients were just fantasizing about their fathers. He then claimed that during development, a child has feelings of desire for their opposite-sex parent and jealousy and anger toward their same-sex parent and called it the Oedipus complex.

When Freud recanted his earlier research findings, he effectively denied women's traumatic realities. That denial persisted within the field for decades until sufficient numbers of women reopened the subject. In the 1970s, researchers in traumatic stress began including victims of domestic violence and sexual assault. Chipping away at gender biases in patient care, they observed similarities in trauma symptoms across the board. This focus was followed by another interest to women in the field—the study of trauma among children.

UNDERLYING CHILDHOOD TRAUMA

In the mid-1980s, Dr. Vincent Felitti was working with adult diabetes patients in his medical clinic. He set out to help them change their diets and increase exercise to lose weight. Most of them got off to an enthusiastic start and then either dropped out or failed to achieve goals. Dismayed by their overall lack of progress, he set up individual interviews with each participant and reviewed their history. He discovered that participants who were victims of childhood abuse and particularly sexual abuse (i.e., people with early trauma) used eating as a way to handle negative emotions and modulate their dysregulated distress responses. The more negative experiences they had in childhood, the worse their health outcomes. Realizing the significance in his research, he joined forces with a colleague, Robert Anda from the Centers for Disease Control and Prevention, to build a larger study. The Kaiser Foundation helped them develop a survey for over seventeen thousand patients that became known as the Adverse Childhood Experiences (ACEs) study. The results showed that people with abuse, neglect, and family household trauma had poor physical health outcomes (such as cancer, heart disease, stroke, and diabetes) and poor mental health outcomes (such as panic disorder and depression in adulthood). Early traumatic experiences make people less resilient adults.

FAMILY TRAUMA AND EPIGENETICS

Family therapists and other mental health professionals began using the ACEs scale to assess their client's traumatic histories. Family therapists are experts in family systems and good at connecting the dots. They are able to identify current traumatic incidents that link back to prior unhealed traumatic experiences.

With a rise in the field of epigenetics (the study of how behaviors and the environment change the ways genes work), a person's trauma history became even more relevant to symptomology. Evidence has been found that trauma changes the DNA in the offspring of trauma survivors and changes regions in the brain that manage the central nervous system during intense fear.

Neuroimaging shows that after repeated fear-inducing experiences, the amygdala (the brain's trauma response center) changes in volume and reactivity. An overactive amygdala sets up vulnerability to traumatic stress and is predictive of PTSD. Over time, biological adaptations help us survive another day and live to produce offspring. The brain has neuroplasticity, and when flooded with multiple traumatic stressors, it changes so we are even more alert for danger, quicker to run for cover, better at fighting off attacks, and when necessary, more adept at playing dead. This overactive alert system can then be inherited by subsequent offspring. The body's genetics change to guarantee the species' survival, but the payoff comes at a great emotional cost—hypervigilance, chronic anxiety, sleeplessness, and dissociation.

TRANSGENERATIONAL EFFECTS

Studies in transgenerational trauma due to racial oppression and violence further broadened and informed individual patient care. I will explore generational trauma and cultural trauma care later in the book. But for now, think for a minute about people who have inherited generational trauma. Indigenous people in America, Holocaust survivors, immigrant communities, and Black families have all had trauma passed down through generations. Did you consider White coal mining communities in Appalachia? Did you think about dust bowl migrants or families who have lived in poverty for three or more generations?

When America was birthed, as is well described by Resmaa Menakem in his book *My Grandmother's Hands*, White settlers were generational trauma survivors. They came to this country to establish "safe" harbors after escaping genocide and religious persecution. In the early American colonies, European immigrants perpetuated brutality against one another. For example, Puritans tortured the Quakers with branding and maiming. As Whites gained wealth and the desire to maintain it, they enslaved Black people from Haiti and the Congo in Africa and directed their violence toward their slaves, resulting in centuries-long White-on-Black violence.

Going back through most family histories of people in America, you will find generational trauma. When we begin hearing and validating the individual trauma stories people share, we find a US history different from the one we learned in school. When we look through a trauma lens, we learn about suffering and pain among our diverse neighbors here in the United States and about our country's trauma legacy. When this trauma is not recognized or healed, violence toward others results. White trauma has been perpetrated against the Black community through enslavement, lynching, Jim Crow laws, land seizure, mass incarceration, health care inequities, and denied voting rights. It underlies White body supremacy and the social caste system in the United States.

Whatever your race, ethnicity, or religious roots, the trauma you think is yours might thread back through a long lineage. Experts in the fields of sociology and psychology are engaging in groundbreaking new work to identify and treat transgenerational traumas. Sociologist Joy DeGruy has developed a term she calls "Post Traumatic Slave Syndrome" to describe traumatic violence in Black history. While this term has not yet been added to the diagnostic manual for mental health providers, it is being used to increase culturally sensitive mental health treatment.

Post Traumatic Slave Syndrome

"Post Traumatic Slave Syndrome . . . is a condition that exists as a consequence of multigenerational oppression of Africans and their descendants resulting from centuries of chattel slavery. A form of slavery which was predicated on the belief that African Americans were inherently/genetically inferior to whites. This was then followed by institutionalized racism which continues to perpetuate injury."[2]–Joy DeGruy

DeGruy's work has expanded clinicians' viewpoints about racial trauma and shown that no individual with trauma can be entirely freed from their ancestral roots. Therapists now regularly look back through their patients' histories to locate, identify, and formulate plans to heal culturally inherited and racialized individual trauma.

YOUR INDIVIDUAL TRAUMA

I was senior pastor in a church where I preached each week, receiving typical affirming comments in the greeting time after the service. But I've never forgotten a member of the board who made a comment about my sermon one week. "Well, pastor," she said. "This morning you left off preaching and began meddling!" Let this story be a warning to you that I'm about to start meddling with you—if meddling means that I awaken you to the trauma you carry inside your body and soul so you can find healing and peace.

Exploring Your Own Trauma

To expand and deepen your work in trauma care, I invite you to begin a journal describing your trauma history. Go back through your individual and family history and take notes about traumatic events and what followed them. Ask trusted family members to join you in your exploration.

To improve your pastoral care and reduce the risk of harming victims, it is essential that you keep unhealed trauma from interfering in your work. Unhealed trauma could reduce your ability to stay calm and grounded alongside others in a traumatic situation. By unearthing trauma experiences in your past, getting help, and healing, you will better be able to stay present and compassionate. Consider finding a trauma-informed therapist now to help you with prior and current traumatic situations.

Competent clergy regularly consult therapists in person or online to discuss complicated pastoral relationships. An interpersonal conflict that appears to be puzzling, emotionally charged, or making a big deal about nothing may have underlying systemic or personal trauma within it. Asking a professional to help you sort that out can greatly enhance your effectiveness in ministry and reduce burnout. Waiting until a crisis erupts or becomes rigidly conflicted is sadly all too common. Plan now to get the help and support you need from someone who understands and treats trauma.

Your list of personal traumatic experiences will grow longer as you read through this book. If, when putting things on the list, you notice changes in your breathing and heart rate, this is a sign that you are being triggered. In that case, put down your pen or pencil and see what happens when you do the breathing exercises I've been suggesting. By noticing sensations and changes in your body and taking deep, slow breaths, you can reverse the body's adrenaline rush during these exercises.

Dropping In

Thinking about trauma can awaken your sympathetic nervous system. To slow it down, take three to five deep breaths and soften your eye gaze or close your eyes. Pull up the word relax *into your field of vision, as if this word just scrolled like a screen saver across your computer monitor. Take a few more breaths, and on the out breath, make an audible sigh. This practice is called "dropping in" and takes us to a place of greater stillness and relaxation. Do this as long and as often as you need to.*

If you find that exploring your traumatic history is in any way unsettling, you may want to make or review your trauma list under the guidance of a trauma-informed therapist. Such therapists follow these practices:

- establish safe therapeutic relationships based on compassion and acceptance
- monitor their client's storytelling and look for avoidance, shame, or dissociation
- see trauma-related symptoms as normal and help clients with negative self-talk or shame regarding their coping mechanisms
- believe that full recovery is achievable[3]

An important reason for you to explore and address your own experiences of trauma is to avoid what therapists call "countertransference," the unconscious projection of your emotional issues onto those you care for. If you aren't aware of your countertransference, you might find yourself daydreaming, rubbing your palms together, feeling jittery, distracted by noises, or even yawning and feeling very tired. When you experience these symptoms of trauma arousal, it will become more difficult for you to concentrate or even hear what another person is saying, and you might "check out" emotionally. By learning to recognize these physical symptoms as they arise and start interfering, you can shift them. You can breathe deeply, change your sitting position, or use mindfulness techniques in order to remain present, loving, and compassionate.

Trauma Transference

In therapy, transference refers to a relational dynamic wherein patients naturally project their feelings for significant person(s)–such as parents, partners, and children–onto their therapist. Countertransference takes place when the therapist's unfinished relational dynamics are projected onto their patients in return. The term more generally describes an emotional entanglement with a patient.

A HEURISTIC APPROACH

In the field of scientific discovery, there are different learning methods. One of them is known as a heuristic, a term borrowed from a Greek word that means "I find, or I discover." Psychologists consider heuristics a valid method of discovery. They value personal stories and self-examination. As we consider trauma-informed care, I invite you to begin your own heuristic journey, and I will share one of my heuristic stories to get you started.

Twenty years after my seventeen-year first marriage ended, I reached out to a trauma-informed therapist and asked him to treat the secondary trauma I was picking up in my work. Taking a brief history, he paused and said, "You went through a traumatic divorce!" I was thrown off base. Was it *traumatic*? Had I minimized its impact? True, there were emotional triggers I still felt when hearing about or seeing my ex-husband, but . . . seeing the incredulity on my face, he asked me to describe the way it ended.

I reluctantly began. A week after my husband suddenly announced his plan to divorce me, I received a threatening certified letter from his lawyer. I soon faced the loss of half of my parenting time with my preteen daughter. Within six months, I had to move out of the home we shared, change jobs, and start life over again.

As I allowed the story to emerge, an old, buried memory came up clearly in my mind. I was having dinner in my newly found rental house. I hadn't yet gone to the grocery store, and my daughter was at her dad's. I poured myself a glass of flat champagne from a bottle I'd kept in the fridge after a friend came over and opened it with me, insisting I'd be better off in the long run. I found a can opener and a spoon in an unpacked kitchen box and opened a can of beef stew. I ate it cold and swigged the champagne to help it go down.

That night, my insufficient "meal" was all I could manage. My body had absorbed the trauma. But I didn't want to focus on the pain. I wanted to think of myself as strong and focus on surviving. Still, I was on my way to losing thirty pounds. I was on a downward spiral that didn't slow down until a colleague who cared deeply about me told me to set my dining table with my best china (I'd kept that in the divorce), a tablecloth my mom had embroidered, and my grandmother's silverware. She told me to buy myself flowers at the market and prepare a healthy, wonderful meal from scratch as if I were entertaining royalty. "Because you are worth it!" she said, nearly shouting at my inertia in exasperation. I heard her message, and it reaffirmed God's claim on my life at my baptism: "You are my beloved, with whom I am well pleased." Like Jesus in the Jordan River, it was time for me to come up out of the water.

After telling this story to my new therapist (more than twenty years later), I was clearly still in denial. "I'm over it," I told him. "I'm in a wonderful marriage; my daughter and I are both happy." He was patient with my attempts to reframe and minimize the experience. He could also tell that my trauma was still hiding out in memories too deep to access by logic or reasoning. They were lodged, as all traumas are, in my body without my consent.

Therapist Deb Dana, who studies the neurobiology within trauma, notes, "Trauma is both a psychological and a physical experience that impacts our internal sense of safety and our ability to trust in self, in relationships, and the world."[4] Trying to keep going and serving my church took every bit of relational energy I had. The church had been through a major trauma before I arrived, and though I didn't know it then, I now see that we began our ministry walking together in shock.

My divorce left me profoundly shaken, and by denying the way it affected me, I survived and thrived thereafter. Eventually, though, I had to reclaim my trauma story in order to be less reactive and more effective in my care for others. Processing this trauma built a thicker fire wall around my mind and spirit so that new traumatic material couldn't burn through it as quickly.

It Was Terrible, but Was It Trauma?

As you make your trauma list, don't worry about technical definitions. There are experiences that make us say, "Yes, of course. Trauma with a capital *T*" (a near plane crash, a concert where gunfire broke out, a family member in detention at the border). But in other situations, we might call them traumas with a small t. Be aware that people are more likely to deny trauma experiences than overreport them. Just keep writing things down as you recall them. For our purposes, do not limit your list to times when you may have received a trauma diagnosis. But rest assured, there is no shame in having had one.

COMMON SYMPTOMS

How is trauma diagnosed? When someone has clusters of symptoms, mental health professionals use those to assign diagnostic terms for medical billing and treatment. Traumatic stress is diagnosed as acute stress disorder during the first month after trauma and posttraumatic stress disorder (PTSD) thereafter.

Symptoms of these disorders are clustered into categories that can be found in the American Psychiatric Association *Diagnostic and*

Statistical Manual of Mental Disorders, known as *DSM-5*. (The 5 refers to the most recent edition.) But here is a summary of adult symptoms:

- *Intrusion:* experiencing intrusive memories, dreams, distress, reactions to internal or external cues, and dissociation
- *Avoidance:* avoiding thoughts and feelings associated with trauma and avoiding external reminders
- *Negative mood and cognition:* thinking negatively, having distorted or fragmented memories, focusing on negative emotions (e.g., fear, horror, anger, guilt, shame), experiencing social withdrawal, and feeling detached or estranged
- *Changes in arousal and reactivity:* losing sleep, having problems concentrating, being easily startled, displaying reckless or self-destructive behavior, feeling irritable, feeling anger without provocation, and displaying verbal and physical aggression[5]

Not all symptoms are necessarily present in each category, and clinicians use other criteria as well. They ask, for example, how bothersome are these symptoms (what is the patient's subjective distress level)? How many symptoms does this person have? How long do they last? Trauma symptoms can continue for a long time, although 50 percent of people find that their symptoms have gone away within three months. When people have complex trauma (due to repeated or overlapping traumatic incidents), it may take many months or even years to heal. Rarely, prolonged trauma can last as long as fifty years.[6]

If you have some of the symptoms listed here, please know that you are not alone. Most symptoms are common and treatable. In the aftermath of the Covid-19 pandemic (more than a year of prolonged fear and anxiety), many people have lingering trauma symptoms. Be aware that your mental health and your physical health may have deteriorated in that stressful time. When your body perpetually activates the sympathetic nervous system, it can lead to chronic hypertension, digestive inflammation, and autoimmune disorders. To make diagnosis even trickier, nearly sixty common medical problems present with psychological symptoms. Make sure you have a doctor's appointment for any new or worsening physical or mental health symptoms.

IS EVERY TRAUMATIC EXPERIENCE DEVASTATING?

We are all impacted differently by trauma, and some of us are more likely than others to end up with trauma symptoms after a tragedy. Here's the good news: research has conclusively shown that nearly 80 percent of individuals who go through a single traumatic event do not go on to develop long-term symptoms or be diagnosed with PTSD. Unfortunately, people with multiple traumatic wounds do not fare as well. Some people experience what I call "trauma loading"— prior traumatic personal or familial experiences that increase vulnerability to negative outcomes. People who carry a load of trauma with them from childhood or from constant life-threatening situations in adulthood will have a more difficult time managing subsequent traumas. People who endure repeated traumatic threats will have greater challenges managing physiological arousal in their bodies. Based on these and other vulnerabilities, traumatic events affect each person differently.

Exploring Your Bias

Look around at the people in your congregation or with whom you work and serve. Which people are most likely to be trauma resilient? Which people are less likely to be trauma resilient, and why? Would you determine this by their skin or hair color, their clothing, their gender conformity or nonconformity, the look on their face, or the assistive devices they use? Considering your presumptions and biases now will help you stay less biased as you care for others.

PRETRAUMA FACTORS

An individual's vulnerability during and after trauma is based on "pretraumatic" factors. When Dr. Felitti explored his patient's histories, he found childhood abuse, neglect, and family disintegration trauma. These conditions make people less able to get back on their feet after a natural disaster, less able to push aside nightmares or return to work after a workplace accident, slower to move beyond daily tears after the loss of a child. People who have experienced these factors are simply more vulnerable to acute stress and face more obstacles in recovery.

Women generally report greater numbers of childhood traumas, one in five having been sexually molested or raped by age twenty-five. Men may have similar rates but are less likely to disclose their trauma during research or therapy. Men report childhood sexual abuse trauma at rates between one in eight and one in ten. Multiple studies suggest that individuals with transgender identities experience abuse trauma at higher rates than either men or women.

After trauma, long-term outcomes depend on the developmental stage of the child at the time they were traumatized. For example, most patients with dissociative personality disorders have been physically and/or sexually abused prior to age six. Early trauma contributes to a disintegration of the building blocks that shape personality, and it leads to the splitting off of subpersonalities. As one victim described her childhood abuse, she said that she made herself "an army" to withstand her brother and his friends' repeated sexual assaults.

Other vulnerable groups include people with mental or physical disabilities and LGBTQ people; these individuals are more likely to have high childhood ACEs scores and trauma from targeted aggressions. In 2019, Dr. Wendy Ellis, director of the Center for Community Resilience, published her remarkable new work on the overlap between ACEs scores on the Kaiser scale and adverse community environments that contribute to poor health outcomes. Childhood poverty, incarcerated parents, food and housing insecurity, inadequate health care, and racial oppression all add to the early trauma of many people who carry these insecurities forward into their adulthood.

Mental Health Prior to Trauma

Another pretraumatic factor contributing to trauma vulnerability is having poorer than average mental health when trauma hits. When people are evaluated for PTSD, they are typically asked about previous clinical diagnoses. This makes sense. One or more preexisting mental health condition can make it even harder to overcome trauma. During Covid-19, for example, people with prior disorders such as panic or anxiety disorder, depression, suicidality, and obsessive-compulsive disorder had a greater vulnerability to exacerbated symptoms under lockdown.

Clergy helping parishioners stay positive during the pandemic were often puzzled by people's extreme moods and fears. People who refused to wear masks expressed fear of losing their freedom, and people who wore masks were more afraid of catching the virus. But people who had contagion fear and cleaned or sanitized obsessively before Covid-19 found it especially difficult to manage their symptoms.

A seventy-year-old man in my extended family encountered an unmasked stranger in the grocery aisle. He asked the man to put on a mask, and when the man refused, he held up his walker like a lion tamer uses a stool and pushed the man back to a safer distance. Was he in a "normal" state of anxiety or in triggered trauma? Did past traumatic material increase his hypervigilance or help him accurately assess the threat level? Many individuals who were arrested for breaking into the Capitol building were war veterans. I believe that there is a connection between their past traumatic experiences and their reactions that day. Trauma, whether conscious or unconscious, influences our thoughts and behaviors in highly stressful circumstances. Unhealed trauma can erupt in violence, and violence can expose unhealed trauma.

Diagnostic Bias and Shame

To help trauma victims, trauma-informed clergy consider each victim's present and past interpersonal and social environments. That being sound practice, I also encourage you to avoid applying diagnostic labels. While it took more than eighty years to develop these categories by identifying symptom clusters, it is an imperfect system that too often focuses on individuals rather than context. Diagnostic categories fail to identify symptoms resulting from injustices within gender, race, and class violence. Categories are also applied in a biased manner. Women are more often diagnosed with dependent personality disorder and borderline personality disorder than men. Black and Latinx clients are diagnosed with schizophrenia three to four times more often than Caucasians who present identical symptoms.

What's Going on Here?

An ordinary daily exchange between two individuals can set off traumatic vulnerability. When a Black man gets into an elevator, he sees a woman gripping her purse a little tighter and backing away from him. He sees fear in her eyes despite the smile she quickly offers. Is he accurately reading his threat level when he is around a White woman who has been taught to fear him? Is she accurately responding to a threat or flooded with a fear she's been taught?

She won't likely go to a therapist to find out why her heart rate increased or why she broke into a sweat when she saw him. If she did, would the therapist look into her history and assign her a diagnosis? Would the therapist know how to help her with her ingrained racism?

He could be reluctant to seek therapy, and rightly so, if reporting his repeated experiences with racial macroaggressions resulted in a diagnosis of paranoia permanently added to his medical file. Considering centuries of violence against Black men for talking to or making eye contact with White women, he was physically and mentally responding with a totally appropriate level of heightened awareness and need for self-protection. A culturally sensitive and unbiased therapist might diagnose him with chronic traumatic stress or not assign a diagnosis at all.

As a matter of good professional ethics, every person providing emotional support needs to consider bias. The lens through which we operate has been culturally formed and shaped by racism, privilege, patriarchy, class, and religious discrimination. Diagnostic labels are inherently based on cisgender, heterosexual, White-bodied "normalcy." A mental health diagnosis can have lasting negative consequences for employment, economic advancement, housing, and parenting rights. Why do we use them at all? The next version of the *DSM* will hopefully consider a more fluid and culture/race sensitive approach.

I got a phone call from a potential client at my therapy office. She told me her first name and then said, "And I hope you can work with me. I was sexually abused by my uncle from age ten to fourteen, I have panic disorder, depression, an eating disorder, and borderline personality disorder." I paused to let her breathe. By God's grace, I am sometimes prompted to say the right thing. I asked her, "If we strip away those diagnoses, who else are you?" There was silence on the line. I took some slow deep breaths myself and then said, "If we work together, I want you to come in here without those labels. Come in with your pain, your hopes, your defeats, and your successes. Bring your past, your current problems, and your future goals." It was a risky thing to say. Could she set aside the labels, the disempowering list of symptoms, the "crazy" stigma? She heard me. I agreed to treat her, and we had nearly two years together in which she found her true self, buried beneath the rubbish pile of categorical restrictions that other providers heaped on her. Her diagnoses didn't define her worth; there was so much more to her, awaiting grace and liberation.

A FAITH-BASED VIEWPOINT

The diverse people around you, both resilient and challenged, need your compassion. As clergy, you can offer support without diagnostic labels—with more grace and less shame. You can come alongside people with a firm belief that they can and will recover. Trauma-informed clergy start from this premise: Every person we encounter is a child of God.

Picture the faces among the people in your congregation when they gather for worship. Look at everyone as both resilient and vulnerable. Then imagine asking people in those chairs or pews to stand up if they'd been impacted by traumatic circumstances and begin to name those traumas (domestic violence, sexual abuse, military combat, gun violence, natural disasters, and lastly the pandemic). Before long, I'm pretty sure they would all be standing. If they felt safe enough to push past their shame, they would feel accepted and validated, wouldn't they? Look out there again in your imagination and tell them that no matter where they are in their healing, they are all beloved and all survivors! Use your own words, but whatever you do, offer them grace.

CHAPTER FOUR
TRAUMATIC GRIEF
PROLONGED AND DELAYED MOURNING

O Lord, you have searched me and known me. . . .
For it was you who formed my inward parts;
you knit me together in my mother's womb. . . .
In your book were written
all the days that were formed for me,
when none of them as yet existed.

—Psalm 139:1, 13, 16

Here's how we learn human attachment: Our parents have sex, our cells divide, and our bodies develop, bathed in our mother's life-giving amniotic fluids. After we are born, we retain some of our mothers' cells and leave her with some of ours. The cells we exchange will be in our bodies until we die. Meanwhile, we learn to look into adoring eyes, we experience closeness and safety while being held by dear ones, and we develop finely tuned cranial neurons that detect emotions and feel similar emotions in return. From this first reciprocity, we learn to love and connect.

The power of these human attachment bonds becomes even more evident when love is withheld, withdrawn, or severed. We so crave human companionship that we grow angry when we feel abandoned and alone, and we grieve, perhaps inconsolably, when a loved one dies. We instinctually need others for safety, comfort, and validation. When these bonds are severed, we feel pain. Brain imagery shows that this pain is so intense that it can be compared to surgery without anesthesia.

DISRUPTED GRIEF

It's the fall of 2020, and I am leaving the hospital after visiting a dear friend. There's only one way in and one way out of this sprawling facility due to Covid-19 precautions, so I keep my distance and wait by the elevators for people in the hallway to clear out.

A bottleneck has formed with people entering the building. At the head of the line stands a weary looking woman in her late forties carrying a huge cellophane-wrapped bunch of sunflowers, carnations, and orchids. Close behind her stands a tall, prematurely balding man with an oversized box of Costco cookies in his arms. The woman says something I can't hear to the front desk attendant, who is young and likely in her first job. She acts not the least bit interested in the woman's story. She shakes her head without looking at the woman and says, "You can't go up there, ma'am." The lobby quiets down as the woman's face sinks, and I see that she is crying. The man puts his hand on her shoulder to comfort her or pull her back; I can't tell which. She finds her voice: "My mom died in this hospital yesterday after three weeks here. I just want to thank the nurses and doctors who cared for her."

The clerk turns her back on the woman and shuffles some papers on her desk. I can feel the woman's trauma in my body, and I'm getting angry. So I break protocol and move closer to the desk clerk. I say to her, "This would be a good time to call the chaplain's office. Maybe the chaplain could work something out and find a way to help them with what they need."

Everyone is still silent. The young woman looks angry now, as if everyone in the lobby is going to join forces and attack her. She turns toward me, red-faced, raises her voice in self-defense, and repeats the script: "Well, they can't go up there!"

I wait to see if she calls the chaplain, but she waves the next people in line to come on through the logjam and dismisses the whole thing. The woman with the flowers is crying harder as the man gently backs her away from the entrance. I pass through the front door to a welcome slap of cold air on my face. By the time I reach my car, I am crying too.

What's Going on Here?

The young desk clerk's central nervous system is going into fight/flight/freeze, so she disconnects from the woman's emotions through what is called dissociation. Her body instructs her to take immediate action and get this over with as quickly as possible. When she feels challenged and becomes scared and angry, she also becomes cognitively inflexible. "Let me think this over and find a solution" is the farthest thing from her mind. Her frontal lobes have shut down, and she is operating out of what is often called her reptilian brain. She may not have even heard my comment, because an activated central nervous response dulls the normal sound of human voices and heightens awareness about predatory noises like high pitches and low growls. She either doesn't hear me or doesn't know what to do with my comment. She just knows she has a job to do.

Months later, as I think about the front desk clerk, I still feel angry at her, more for her callousness than for enforcing the rules. This is my trauma response, retriggered when I recall the story. I have to settle myself down to find empathy for her. I have to step away from the scene and get curious about it in order to recognize her response as trauma, pushed down. I stood in the lobby just once, while she was there every day for months, encountering hostile patrons who didn't like mask wearing protocols and stood too close. When I dial back my fight response, I settle my brain down and empathize rather than stay angry. I see that she had to remain emotionally disconnected. She may never have had a personal grief experience from which to build empathy. Had she opened her heart to these people, it would have derailed her. Denial was necessary. It paid her bills.

TRAUMATIC GRIEF

This scene represents just one among millions of attachment bonds that were broken during the pandemic. Covid-19 separated the woman from her very sick mother in the days and last hours before she died, when ordinarily they would have held hands, and the daughter would have touched her mother's face and said gently, "I love you." And after her mother died, she would have lingered in the room a while to say good-bye. Instead, she was overwhelmed with grief, as were the families of half a million people who died during the first twelve months of the pandemic in the United States. At that point, one in three people in the United States knew someone who had died of Covid-19. The enormity of grief during the pandemic will change how we look at trauma and grief recovery over the next few decades.

Traumatic Grief

Traumatic grief is a relatively new term describing an individual's distress in reaction to the loss of a loved one in traumatic circumstances, including sudden, violent, self-inflicted, or otherwise unnatural deaths. Traumatic loss is itself a separation trauma. Still under study by the American Psychiatric Association, traumatic bereavement varies depending on "the deceased's last moments, degree of suffering and mutilating injury, or the malicious or intentional nature of the death."[1]

Covid-19 deaths fit this category of losses in traumatic circumstances, leaving millions of Americans to rebuild their lives in the decade after. They are simultaneously going through trauma recovery and grief recovery. Traumatic grief is characterized by feelings of abandonment, yearning to make meaning from senseless loss, spiritual reckonings and recalculations, loneliness, and interpersonal isolation. Persons in traumatic grief may feel numb, unsafe, distrusting, angry, and futile as they go through the grief process. Families who lose primary wage earners may face the subsequent traumatic stressors of poverty, hunger, and eviction, delaying their recovery for months or years.

If traumatic grief continues beyond twelve months, it is called persistent complex grief disorder. Symptoms include reactive distress such as difficulty accepting a loved one's death, emotional numbness, anger or bitterness, social disruption and interpersonal detachment, feeling life is meaningless and empty, and difficulty pursuing former interests. Other symptoms include difficulty finding positive memories to hold on to and suicidality due to a strong desire to be with a deceased loved one.[2] The long-term mental health impacts of traumatic grief during the pandemic will last years beyond medical advancements in treatments and vaccinations for the Covid-19 virus and its variants.

The Breath Hold

Before reading the next section, take three or four deep breaths for relaxation. Breathe in through your nose and out through your mouth. Remember to count longer on the out breath than on the in breath. On your next out breath, extend the "pause" and gently hold your breath, comfortably allowing stillness between breaths. These breath-holding moments stop ruminating thoughts. Simply relax in those few moments without effort as the mind comes into stillness. Try pausing and extending the hold after the out breath a few more times. These pauses literally disrupt your busy brain's usual reactivity and offer moments of mental rest.

DISPROPORTIONATE SUFFERING

The pandemic resulted in people grieving traumatic deaths in multigenerational family clusters and communities. People died at exponentially higher numbers in ravaged tribal communities, senior care facilities, multigenerational Latinx and Black families, and Orthodox Jewish communities. Since the Spanish flu, which killed 675,000 people, no other tragedy has created as many losses or as much grief in the United States.

Due to inequitable medical treatment and vaccination distribution among Native American, Black, and Latinx people in the United States during the pandemic, whole communities were devastated by multiple deaths. These populations have historically borne traumatic losses in America through forced migrations, persistent racial violence, and the denial of access to adequate health care. Each culture expresses grief differently through traditions that include both private and public rituals, and yet these three groups share some characteristic responses to transgenerational oppression. They rely on church affiliation and community interconnectivity to foster resiliency.

Many American descendants of slavery (ADOS) and other Black people in the United States experience loss and grief frequently and distinctively due to medical mistreatment, police brutality, civil injustices, substance abuse, and incarceration. Many Latinx communities face frequent traumatic losses due to immigration incarcerations and deportations. Both groups turn to the church for cultural preservation and integration with people who share values, beliefs, and traditions.

In a literature review of mental health and religious affiliation in racial and ethnic minority populations, researcher Ann W. Nguyen notes, "Religion has undoubtedly been an important source of resilience for many racial and ethnic minority populations, and its narrative of perseverance and faith has proven to be a sustaining force for these populations in the face of hardships and inequality."[3] People who are accustomed to grief due to centuries of oppression often embrace stoicism in the face of repeated profound losses, and they accept and tolerate suffering. As they grieve, attachment bonds fostered by their Christian communities serve to heal and restore them. In these communities, people help one another with traumatic wounds by affirming their ongoing connections to the departed through dreams, private conversations, visits to cemeteries, and the marking of birthdays and deathdays.

Grieving families help one another through loss by reaching out to church pastors and friends for prayer and spiritual sustenance. The role of the Black church is strongly positive for many individuals and families during grief recovery.[4] The church offers liberation and defiance theologies to help members cope with discrimination and to work for justice reforms. Multiple studies show that in both Black and Latinx families, church attendance lowers depression, substance use, suicidal ideation, and anxiety. According to one researcher, religious affiliation appears to be even more restorative for Black, Indigenous, and people of color (BIPOC) as compared to Whites.[5]

PARTNERSHIPS AND GENDER

The weight of traumatic grief is carried differently and expressed differently according to race, ethnicity, social class, and gender. Along with family norms and religious affiliations, what we have been taught about our assigned gender can shape our behaviors as we go through traumatic grief. While all people feel similar emotions when they grieve, we are also socialized and reinforced to express our emotions differently. Cisgender males are expected to grieve internally, and cisgender females are expected to grieve outwardly. These differences are even more evident in cultures where gender norms are strictly adhered to.

The adage that in times of danger and stress women tend and befriend reflects some truth. The need to protect infants, for example, is at the core of women's central nervous system response when under threat. During traumatic grief recovery, women tend to form deeper and broader bonds to help them with loss and separation, and men are more likely to go through recovery alone, increasing their detachment and drawing upon personal fortitude.

I recall a man I'll call Chet, who was in traumatic grief after his wife, Mary, died in a terrible car accident. He was lost without her after nearly fifty years by her side. He found it hard to sleep, wandered around the house, lost weight, and often found himself losing track of time while staring at her picture. Not accustomed to telling anyone about his feelings, he resisted phone calls and visits. Instead, he threw himself into a project to reroof the steeply pitched sanctuary at a church where I was his pastor. Chet had installed that old roof twenty years earlier. As he pulled out each nail, he revisited his life story—sometimes sighing, sometimes laughing out loud for no reason I could tell, and sometimes cursing at himself for "putting so many damned nails in this roof to begin with." He was cursing the passing of time and the drunk driver responsible for Mary's death. And he was determined to work through his traumatic grief over long hours on the roof.

Differing grief recovery strategies, and differing timelines for grief resolution, can challenge couples regardless of gender or orientation. Will the woman with the flowers and her male companion grow closer during their grief, or will the traumatic components of the loss and delays in resolution due to postponed rituals leave them both feeling alone as they process what happened? Loving connection is restorative and healing, but sadly, many people push one another away in times when they need one another the most. If either partner in a relationship was taught to distrust emotions, they might feel more separate. If either of them watched an elder in their family respond to death as if it didn't happen, that too might shape their grief. They may withdraw from each other, feeling they have nothing to offer. Couples often drift apart as they mourn in the months following a traumatic death, and they need professional help and intervention so they can learn how to turn toward each other as they heal their grief and build a stronger and more secure relationship bond. Clergy can play a helpful role by describing the benefits of professional therapy and making a referral. Couples who stay together and talk about their grief throughout the mending process turn traumatic grief into traumatic growth. During and after trauma, safe relationships are essential to recovery.

Hand Holding

Studies have found that holding the hand of a loved one lowers risk perception during and after trauma by alerting the parasympathetic nervous system to reduce physical arousal and release calming hormones. When fears flood the body, a calm voice can call you back, and the feel of someone's hand can lead you home.

TRAUMATIC GRIEF AND POSTTRAUMATIC STRESS

When grief follows a shocking loss, the survivor's symptoms look similar to traumatic stress disorder symptoms. The bereaved person may experience ruminating thoughts, nightmares, startle responses, and intrusive memories, among other things. This information can help a grieving person to understand their symptoms and gain self-compassion about seemingly "bizarre" and unsettling experiences.

During the pandemic, hospital workers, including physicians, nurses, aids, ambulance drivers, and janitorial staff, faced massive traumatic losses. Chaplains watched many people die each day. Hospital floors became trauma units in both the medical and mental health senses of the word. There was barely enough time to tend to the living, let alone to mourn the dead.

Rabbi Jason Weiner, director of spiritual care at Cedars Sinai Hospital in Los Angeles, told *All Things Considered* reporter Tom Gjelten that their grief "is cumulative, it gets worse and worse, and you feel it. Sometimes you could just be sitting at home, and you hear a siren or something, and it could be a trigger. It's definitely severe. As chaplains we're trying to provide support for the staff, for the patients, and for the families. So it's a triple whammy in some ways."[6]

After long shifts, chaplains and medical staff frequently went home feeling good about a patient's likely recovery only to return the next day and find that the patient had died overnight. Most said they did not feel like heroes; some said they felt like soldiers on the battlefront.

The more traumatic losses people face in rapid succession, the more they are at risk of becoming debilitated by grief. After many losses, grief overwhelms normal coping mechanisms. One of the saddest illustrations of this condition may be the case of Lorna Breen, a traumatized emergency room physician who was so emotionally overwhelmed during the pandemic that she took her own life.[7]

People who worked on the "front lines" experienced shock and immobilization, intense sorrow, difficulty concentrating, disrupted sleep, physical illness, increased substance use, and suicidality. But each person also responded differently to multiple traumatic losses, depending on pretraumatic vulnerability and social context. Individuals who lacked adequate social support, had multiple traumatic childhood experiences, and who couldn't or didn't access mental health interventions were more challenged. As the pandemic dragged on, some of them decided to leave the field altogether.

Preliminary research reported in the *Journal of Loss and Trauma* during the pandemic shows the overlap between traumatic grief and PTSD. Using validated self-report measures, the authors explored stress reactions among people who had gotten Covid-19, who had a loved one die of Covid-19, or whose job involved Covid-19. Among these three groups, the overall rate of PTSD was 39 percent, which is much higher than the typical 3.5 percent found in the general population. Covid-19 stress was "a strong and statistically significant predictor of posttraumatic stress overall and PTSD symptoms clusters including intrusions, avoidance, negative alterations in cognitions and mood and hyperarousal."[8]

Flipping the statistics over, I want to note that this study concludes that amazingly, more than half of people (61 percent) who were personally impacted by Covid-19 did not indicate that they had PTSD symptoms. Hopefully, they were not underreporting symptoms but were instead confident, strong, and resilient. Some survivors talk about sweet and tender moments in the midst of loss. These memories help them to heal, and many of them have now found ways to express gratitude to hospital staff who cared for their loved ones.

THE HEALING BEGINS

The daughter of Dick and Shirley Meek took her grief into the public spotlight by telling their family story to reporters. Her focus on the blessings during her parents' last hours shows that she is on the road to healing. As hard as loss can be, it can also be tender and holy.

Not many months after celebrating their seventieth wedding anniversary, Dick and Shirley both fell ill to Covid-19 and were hospitalized at a rural community hospital. When they became critically ill, a transfer was ordered for them. "At the time there was a chance that they would be transferred to separate hospitals," their daughter Debbie said, but the staff helped to advocate for them, and they were transferred together.

As their health declined and it became clear that they would not survive, the family asked that they be moved into a room together. "We didn't want them to be separated, because that was their biggest thing in life that they would be together," Debbie said. The staff worked with the family to help them at the end, making a playlist of their favorite songs so they could listen while they held hands for the last time. According to Debbie, when Shirley died, "The nurse put my mom's head on my dad's shoulder . . . and she rubbed my dad's shoulder and said, 'Dick, you can go now. Shirley's waiting for you,'" and within minutes, Dick was gone.[9]

The family was consoled by the diligent patient care and advocacy shown by the staff. The story illustrates the best care in a terrible situation and the way the daughter was comforted by her participation in her parents' end-of-life needs. This was, sadly, not possible in many hospitals.

Clergy and chaplains who witnessed one tragic loss after another honored and maximized the connections families needed. They made video calls on their own phones, rustled up tablets, and created quiet moments amid the crazy noise in intensive care units to help thousands of families across the United States say good-bye.

Debbie's healing story about her parents includes gratitude as well as grief, and I think back to the woman at the start of this chapter who simply wanted to thank the staff who cared for her mother. Survivors need to tell their stories, and as preachers and teachers, we need to pass those stories around. Grief connects us to one another and honors the depth of pain we justifiably feel after each good-bye.

People who have strong ties in faith communities, responsive partners, empathetic loved ones, and healthy relationships with other survivors will build trust and bond again during trauma grief recovery. As trauma-informed clergy, your role is to provide safe places in which to mourn, light candles, cry a thousand tears, and welcome survivors' stories. In the next chapter, we will further explore the role of faith communities in healing traumatic grief.

CHAPTER FIVE
CULTURAL CONSIDERATIONS IN GRIEF CARE

Embrace us, Loving Spirit, when our hearts break. Make yourself fully known to us so that we never feel abandoned or alone. We lament the incalculable numbers of lives lost in the pandemic and in other tragic circumstances. We grieve lost mentors, tribal elders, teachers, frontline workers, health care professionals, clergy, and neighbors. We grieve lost friends, partners, spouses, children, grandparents and parents—so great a cloud of witnesses both nearby and around the world. Grant us grace to stand with those in great pain, humility to learn from one another's grief, and courage to advocate for oppressed and marginalized people.

Grief is a process often left unfinished. Family members, stunned by the Covid-19 virus's swiftness, postponed funerals and other rituals that would have connected them to their extended families and cultural roots. Perhaps they paid tribute to their loved one on Zoom but had to forego the many personal storytelling moments that typically happen at the graveside or in a church, temple, roundhouse, or mosque social hall. They missed hearing candid stories and having private conversations with people who could not be there in person. They missed going to a family home to share traditional foods and line up for photos. Without drumming or dancing or hearing their elders' stories, their grief was disrupted. They didn't get to cry in dozens of loving arms. These lost rituals made the trauma worse.

For many years after Covid-19 and its variants, faith communities will be helping people heal from these traumatic wounds. Clergy will be shaping new rituals for people whose traditional rituals around death were painfully disrupted. We will be scattering ashes with families, holding in-person celebrations, and placing plaques in their memorial gardens to honor their family members and their members' loved ones.

Every person who died left nine or more grieving loved ones behind. As clergy, we are frequently called upon to hear tender, sad, and traumatic stories. Other people's griefs move us, and without drawing attention to ourselves, we sometimes cry alongside them. We weep as Jesus wept. As we listen, we are not just remembering similarly painful experiences in our own lives; we are engaging our brain's perceptive response system.

Mirror Neurons

Our brains are equipped with mirror neurons. These specialized receptors awaken similarly whether we perform an activity or observe someone else performing the same activity. When we observe someone crying, similar feelings are evoked (mirrored) in us, and we feel strongly empathic. People with too many activated mirror neurons can feel overwhelmed by someone else's pain, and research suggests that individuals on the autism spectrum have fewer mirror neurons with which to emotionally connect.

DELAYED GRIEF

When circumstances are such that people postpone their grief, they may experience pain and anguish for weeks or emerge later with displaced emotions or changed behaviors. Sometimes months after a loved one's traumatic death, grief floods over victims with distressing memories, sleep-disrupting dreams, derealization, and flashbacks. Pain can come up unexpectedly and take over cognitive and emotional functioning. Victims of traumatic grief may return to life's tasks, work, and tending to their children and they think they are moving on, only to find themselves overwhelmed again. Trauma-informed clergy may be the first to notice behavioral changes in those who are weighed down by grief and the first to refer people to grief groups and individual mental health providers.

Victims of traumatic grief during the pandemic and other types of traumatic griefs such as combat, gun violence, domestic violence, car crashes, and racially motivated killings may live in fight/flight/freeze states for months and become physically exhausted or ill. Trauma-informed clergy don't shy away from these victims or their pain and instead reach out to them. When people lose one or more safe and loving connections, they can eventually be healed by other attached relationships.

A caring clergyperson can observe and support a parishioner's healing process at any time because traumatic grief recovery doesn't follow a predictable pattern or timeline. The typical grief journey described by Elisabeth Kübler-Ross (denial, anger, bargaining, depression, acceptance) is not as linear as her theory suggests and has been replaced by newer models. Grief stages don't consistently follow the order in which she listed them and may occur simultaneously. Some people don't cycle through every stage. Psychologist William Worden encourages a more active recovery model that includes accepting the loss, experiencing the pain, adjusting to an environment with the deceased missing, and finding an enduring connection with the deceased while creating a new life.[1]

Many models for grief recovery have been based on an individualistic approach to healing and can't be applied cross-culturally. The fields of psychology and psychiatry are steeped in western developmental models that equate health and maturity with individualism and pathologize dependency. In the United States, dominant (White) culture typically views grief recovery as a personal journey. This is not the case among people from collectivist cultures, and some models fall far short when applied to the hardest hit populations in the pandemic. The Latinx, Native American, and Black communities have all faced disrupted healing rituals that normally promote community and support systems that foster healing after a loved one's death.

Latinx Cultural Impacts

Roughly 20 percent of the United States population is Latinx. During the pandemic, many of these families and their extended families were overwhelmed by traumatic grief. In Latinx cultures, extended family (both living and dead) is the source of growth and healing, and grief rituals are essential for grief recovery. Death and dying rituals shape cultural identity for many Hispanic people. In the United States, these communities are from Mexico, Puerto Rico, Cuba, South America, Central America, and the Dominican Republic. Each culture has its own rites and rituals based on historically rooted faith traditions. They are not monolithic, but there are common practices that occur among the bereaved in America.

Due to the relationship orientation in Latinx cultures, there is a focus on attachment rather than letting go. Scholars observe, "Latino/as hold a general belief that there is a continued relationship between the living and the dead resulting in rituals that honor the relationship."[2] Grief is seen as a spiritual process that connects the living with the dead and maintains the relationship. Rituals at church and at altars at home facilitate this communion. Dia de los Muertos (the Day of the Dead) is an important ritual for remembering and honoring loved ones, but each day also includes a conscious awareness of lost loved ones. Daily prayers, conversations with the dead, and ongoing ancestral family connections are cherished rather than seen as obstacles to "moving on." There is no "closure" to grief because these traditions include an ongoing reciprocal relationship between the living and the dead.

Native and Indigenous Grief

The highest percentage of in-culture deaths in the first year of the pandemic occurred among Native and Indigenous peoples. With over five hundred Native and Indigenous tribes in North America, grief rituals are varied. The spiritual perspectives within these cultures have been shaped by relocations, separations, violence, forced education, and family separation traumas. Across many generations in the United States, spiritual practices outside the "norm" of Christianity were seen by Whites to be devilish and dangerous. Introduced to Christianity through oppressive cultural annihilation, some Native people nevertheless identify as Christians. They follow Jesus and adhere to biblical teachings. Other Native and Indigenous people combine Christianity with ancestral rituals and faith traditions. While diverse cultural origins shape tribal grief rituals, the dead are traditionally honored by storytelling, elder teachings, dances, and drumming.

Grief rituals and ceremonies are shaped in the context of each tribal tradition, interpreted by elders. One psychologist explains, "These spiritual leaders provide guidance for mourners about proper ways to channel their grief. They also assist in the continued journey of the spirit." In the Lakota tradition, the pipe ceremony is an act of healing for the family and community and designed for people to "increase their love for one another." In most Native cultures, those who suffer most profoundly are seen as closer to God and therefore considered to be the most holy.[3]

A young widow from an Indigenous tribe taught me that in her experience, grief is a yearlong process. Maria Yellow Horse Brave Heart, in an excellent resource on traumatic grief, described such a year: "It is our way to mourn for one year when one of our relations enters the Spirit World. Tradition is to wear black while mourning our lost loved one, tradition is not to be happy, not to sing and dance and enjoy life's beauty during mourning times. Tradition is to suffer with the remembering of our lost loved one."[4]

While each tribe has its own identity and rituals, community pain and individual pain are often seen as one, and mourners have obligations to their extended family. This may include a beautiful, elaborate distribution of sacred objects and gifts for each family member many months after a loved one's death. Sacred gifts such as blankets, pipes, and knives are handed down through many generations and given with honor to next generations. These ceremonies bind the community to their past and to their future and cannot be overlooked or abandoned.

Black and African American Grief

People who identify as Black or African American died at twice the rate of Whites during the pandemic in the United States, including in both urban and rural areas and among all age groups.[5] Communities and congregations faced overwhelming amounts of grief. Most Black-bodied people are all too familiar with traumatic loss, and lamentation is a constant feature in their grief and healing processes. During the pandemic when families couldn't hold worship services or other public rituals, millions of people grieved in the streets while protesting the murder of George Floyd and other victims of police brutality. Protests against ongoing racial violence and calls for justice express present-day and past traumatic grief. After the 2015 massacre of nine members at Emanuel African Methodist Episcopal Church in Charleston, South Carolina, poet and essayist Claudia Rankine said, "A sustained state of national mourning for Black lives is called for in order to point to the undeniability of their devaluation."[6]

~

Trauma-informed pastoral care during loss and mourning requires us to dismantle our racist presumptions about grief rituals and healing. What theological beliefs and worship practices will be helpful to those in grief? This will be answered differently by each individual and family. The Christian concept of the communion of saints, for example, supports the idea that believers have ongoing relationships with those who have died and are with God in eternity. Many Christians maintain a connection between the dead and living by the tradition of candle lighting and through the veneration of saints both at home and in the church.

In culture-sensitive care, clergy ask about and honor a variety of traditions and grief expressions. They invite mourners and traditional elders to direct them as they come alongside grieving people. They resist judgments about how people grieve or how long they grieve. They become informed about diverse grief practices and rituals and become aware of biases about grief and mourning within their training and within dominant cultures.

Tonglen

A breathing practice in the Buddhist tradition is called Tonglen, which means "sending and taking." Here's a glimpse of how it works. Rest your mind by taking a few deep breaths as you have learned to do from earlier exercises. With each deep in breath, visualize taking in someone's pain or focus on your own pain. With each out breath, send forth compassion and wellness. Breathe in the pain of those who are ill or dying, those who have lost loved ones, people who are oppressed or in any kind of pain. Instead of turning away from suffering, take it in and then breathe out the "medicine" of compassion. Practice this meditation daily.[7]

BUILDING RELATIONAL CONNECTIONS

Diverse people in your congregation and community struggle with ongoing spiritual needs during extended periods of traumatic grief. Trauma-informed pastoral care includes substantial amounts of designated time to be with congregants grieving lost friends, family members, and neighbors. Sadly, this need is not likely to soon diminish. Building upon your knowledge about traumatic grief, you can turn your awareness into actions. Here are a few starting places for helping grieving congregants:

- Invite members and constituents who have drifted away back into community.
- Gently ask about someone's traumatic grief—especially if you see changed behaviors such as verbal aggression, lapses in concentration, or marked changes in mood.
- Avoid retraumatizing people in grief by placing them in environments where people vocally deny their trauma.
- Validate them and allow them to express the full range of emotions they are experiencing.

- Ask them to teach you about their family rituals around death and to guide you in planning funerals, rites, and burials.
- Create small support groups for them, utilizing local therapists.
- Honor their right to be silent about their losses if they so choose and continue to lift them up in your private prayers.

COMMON MISTAKES

Grieving people may not be ready to talk or reconnect with a faith community the first time they are approached and invited. A common mistake in pastoral grief care would be to stop extending invitations. When reaching out, simply indicate that you or others may reach out again from time to time to offer support and that they can always say no again too!

During pastoral care with grieving couples, you need to stay curious about dynamics between them and set aside gender-biased assumptions. Many couples experience dissonance during grief due to diverse ethnic and cultural experiences, family pressure about how they "should" be doing, and discrepancies in their healing journeys. Let each person in any couple teach you about their grief. Ask them what messages they tell themselves about their traumatic grief. What do they think they "should" think, feel, and do? Help them talk with each other about grief as a normal process, even in an abnormal time.

If you sense or observe verbal hostility between couples or family members, talk with them each separately to be sure that they feel safe in the room together. Ask specifically if there is verbal or physical abuse between them, and if so, refer each one to separate therapists for care. If you learn that there has been domestic violence in their home, do not meet with them to talk about or resolve issues between them. This is a common mistake made by clergy who overestimate their counseling ability or place their desire to help above the actual needs of their parishioners.

One last common mistake is underestimating the vulnerability people feel during grief. Mourners lose solid ground both emotionally and interpersonally. Clergy can help them by providing supportive attachments and becoming transitional objects for them but must be aware that their support could be confused with romantic interest and set clear professional boundaries.

Transitional Objects

Developed by George Winnicot, the term *transitional object* originally described objects children use (teddy bears, blankets, dolls) to lower their anxiety during developmental changes in life. Later theorists broadened this theory to include significant adults who become comfort objects during life transitions. With clear and well-maintained professional boundaries, chaplains and clergy become transitional objects as they stand in for a lost loved one by providing a supportive relationship.

The goal in being someone's transitional object is to support them briefly and then link them to another caring individual who can help them over many weeks and months, such as a therapist or spiritual director. During traumatic grief and multiple-loss grief, people in pain aren't helped when parental figures "fix" things or "handle" things for them. As they grieve, whether for fifteen weeks or fifteen years, they need to be empowered. As a clergy care provider, you have the opportunity to hear them and to offer grace as they find their own solutions, make their plans, and take steps back into wholeness.

CONGREGATIONAL CARE

Chaplain Chris Haughee created a list of key principles for congregations that want to use a trauma-informed approach. This list is based on the Substance Abuse and Mental Health Services Administration (SAMHSA) outline mentioned earlier in the book for trauma-informed clergy. This list applies to congregational care and has been redacted here for publication. If you work with or reside within a faith community, this list can open a dialogue about your "call" to support and heal trauma. Share these principles with leaders in your faith community:

1. *Safety:* The faith community provides physical safety along with emotional and relational safety.
    Is there a structure in place that allows for vulnerable people to feel included and protected within our worshipping community?

2. *Trustworthiness and transparency:* Authenticity is valued, and confidences are kept.
    Do those in ministry leadership appear as people in need of God's grace, just as those they minister to?

3. *Peer support:* The congregation is a place where people can make and deepen friendships.
    Can a traumatized person find a listening ear and be welcomed with others who are walking the same road to recovery, grace, and love?

4. *Collaboration and mutuality:* Ministry to and with traumatized adults and children is a priority.
    Can our faith community work with others—even across ideological and denominational lines—for the betterment of hurting people?

5. *Empowerment, voice, and choice:* Those who are ministered to are given service opportunities.
    Are traumatized people seen as an asset with value and wisdom and fully integrated into the life of our faith community?

6. *Cultural, historical, and gender issues:* The congregation recognizes the unique cultural issues bound up with trauma.
    How do we honor the unique cultural, historical, and gender backgrounds of those we serve?

Using these principles, you will capably align yourself with those in traumatic grief recovery. Extensive research has shown that group affiliation and affiliation with faith communities markedly improves overall mental health by reducing social isolation, making meaning out of suffering, helping individuals find purpose, and providing hope.

Pause a moment to think about people in your area who have been most traumatized during the pandemic and make a plan to reach out to them. In some faith communities, designated parish nurses can help you connect with repeatedly traumatized medical providers and other hospital staff. Enlist and fund local therapists to meet with health care workers in small groups in sacred spaces, away from their hospitals and medical centers, places that felt like "crime scenes" during the Covid-19 pandemic. Forming small support groups for health care providers, local chaplains, and other frontline workers will help them work through their experiences and reduce burnout. Many of them saw death in all its ugliness and faced immense ethical dilemmas. You and your congregation can promote healing by forming partnerships with nonprofit organizations who work for justice and improve health care in underresourced areas.[8]

CREATE HEALING RITUALS

Clergy, priests, shamans, elders, prophets, and other ritual makers are essential to healing after trauma. As one of them, you have the opportunity to collaborate with other faith leaders and plan community-wide memorial services. One pastor offered the streetside garden at her parish to the community with places for memorial notes, flowers, and commemorative stones. Clergy have placed banners in upper windows of urban sanctuaries to witness to their losses. Black Lives Matter flags on church lawns honor victims of police brutality and death disparities within the pandemic.

When you sit down with individuals and families to plan memorials and life celebrating events, begin with the breathing exercises in this chapter. Offer prayer by inviting them to tell you the name they call God. Light a candle on an altar in your office for their loved one. Rather than opening your worship book and offering typical rituals to trauma survivors, invite them to tell you what rituals they need.

Cheryl Forster, a multicultural psychologist, notes that culturally sensitive professionals don't operate from the saying in Leviticus 19:18, "You shall love your neighbor as yourself," or by the text called the "golden rule," "In everything do to others as you would have them do to you" (Matt 7:12). Forster points out that people from other backgrounds and cultures may not want to be treated the way you do. She suggests instead that you listen to others and ask them how *they* want to be treated. In other words, "do unto others as *they* want you to do unto them." This ethic honors and values the "other's" wisdom and tradition.[9] Trauma-informed care requires nonjudgmental listening, a willingness to be told about your racial blind spots, and humility to be taught by others.

IT'S NEVER TOO LATE TO HELP PEOPLE IN GRIEF

I met a widow named Marcy while shaking hands with folks after her first Sunday visit to our congregation. On Monday, she called the front office and asked me to come over to see her soon without explaining her urgency. Before midweek, I was in her living room sitting on a brocade couch, staring up at a large pottery vase on her fireplace mantel.

"I want you to meet Jack," she said. I'd looked around, but no one else was in the room. "Jack," she said again, pointing to the vase. "Jack's ashes."

She smiled warmly, which helped because I was feeling a little tense. "I've been carting Jack around in that vase for fifteen years," she said. "I brought him out west with me from Indiana and put him in the garden for a while, and then I moved in with my kids—boy was that a mistake! Jack didn't like it there either; he was crammed in beside boxes on shelves in the garage. So when I brought him here, I gave him a respectable spot there on the mantel, and I've been looking at him ever since."

I really didn't know what to say, so I took this to mean I should keep silent for a while. I wondered how I was going to fit into her story.

"So now, Jack and I have been talking, and we're ready to scatter his ashes with a ceremony the kids can attend. Can you help us do that?"

I said, "Of course," and we began making plans that fit their needs for closure. A few months later, Jack was scattered in the wind, and his widow, Marcy, joined the church. She and Jack taught me that each person's grief has its own unique and sometimes unexpected time frame. It's never too late to celebrate a life!

I was raised, as many of you were, with time limits about grief, such as how many days you can mourn the loss of a loved one, how long a widow or widower should wait before marrying again, and when someone should "get back to normal." Everyone is also raised with differing obligations to other grieving family members, and I can't help others by placing my expectations on them. I learned most of what I know about grief care from very wise teachers who asked for my help.

As you come alongside people in grief, drop all expectations around services and timelines, and respect in-culture ritual making. Help congregants and community members by coming alongside them with what Zen teachers call "beginners mind," which means dropping preconceived ideas and expectations. See every situation with an open heart and open mind, as if this is the first grieving person you have ever served. God has given you the person you are helping to be your teacher.

WALKING AS JESUS WALKED

People are wounded by traumatic grief every day by being suddenly or violently cut off from beloved relationships. Safe, sure, and healthy relationships mend us. Jesus embodies this truth in nearly every healing story in the Gospels. He heals broken victims. Do you recall the man by the sheep pool lying on his mat waiting for someone to put him in the water (John 5:2-9)? What trauma has afflicted him and left him disabled? How has he become a victim with a story he repeats to anyone who can help him? How many snide remarks do others make about him as they shove him out of the way? How long has he been isolated by his pain? Jesus, with compassion, asks the man to declare his desire to be well and then simply instructs him to take up his mat and walk. The narrative tells us the words but perhaps not the action. I picture Jesus wrapping his arms around the man's waist, hoisting the man up and steadying them both until the miracle takes hold. The place this happened is known as Bethesda, which means the "gate of grace."

In Mark's Gospel (5:21-42), Jesus is lecturing by the sea when a distraught father breaks through the crowd and falls at Jesus's feet. He pleads for Jesus to lay healing hands on his dying daughter. As Jesus and the crowd follow the man to his house, Jesus stops along the way for another wounded person. The woman has been hemorrhaging for years by the time she touches his robe, and he is instantly aware of this. Pushing convention aside, and willing to become "unclean" in the process, Jesus heals her. But by then the little girl has died, and his disciples say they should leave the father alone in his grief. Again, Jesus approaches rather than turns away. He finds the daughter on her bed, takes her hand, and says, "Little girl, get up!" and soon gives her into the arms of her weeping father.

Jesus's healing stories have two parts. He approaches outcasts, lepers, beggars, demon-possessed souls, persons with disabilities, or the gravely ill, and he heals them. And then, he gives them back to their families, places of worship, and communities. The restoration of their bodies is immediately followed by restored relationships. It's amazing that the Gospel writers consistently report these vital second steps. Returning a broken person to the arms of their loved ones, giving the outcast a new community, and reconnecting a lost person to God's love at a house of worship are all key components in trauma healing. Jesus's healing stories show us the essence of trauma-informed care.

Theologian Howard Thurman describes this Christlike care in his poem "For a Time of Sorrow" from his book *Meditations of the Heart*:

I share with you the agony of your grief,
> The anguish of your heart finds echo in my own.
> I know I cannot enter all you feel,
> Nor bear with you the burden of your pain;
I can but offer what my love does give:
> The strength of caring,
> The warmth of one who seeks to understand
> The silent storm-swept barrenness of so great a loss,
This I do in quiet ways,
> That on your lonely path
> You may not walk alone.[10]

Thurman's poem points to the balance needed in trauma-informed grief care. He doesn't presume to know what another person could be feeling, but it does echo in his soul. God has provided us with wise bodily connections to others by way of mirror neurons in the brain. When sadness is felt, we know the feeling of sadness; when tears are shed, our eyes fill with tears. And without distraction from our own resonant trauma, it is our job to stay in the experience of the wounded one. "I offer you," Thurman says, "the strength of caring, the warmth of one who seeks to understand." He isn't in his own trauma when he says this; his brain is awake and aware. Christlike, he walks alongside another on a lonely path. This loving connection relieves grief's agony.

CHAPTER SIX
NATURAL DISASTER CARE
INDIVIDUAL AND SYSTEMIC ISSUES

Bless the earth, and all of us upon it, loving Creator. Hot winds swirl chaotically over our endangered planet. Polar ice melts, oceans rise, mountains slide into the seas, frozen lands become uninhabitable, fires explode, and water becomes scarce. We grieve for the planet, for animals and birds, and for the polluted earth our children and their children will inherit. We seek your strength, prophetic passion, and healing grace so we can faithfully and justly restore the earth for all who inhabit it. Amen.

Faith leaders are being called into disaster service as population growth and climate change lead to increasing numbers of hurricanes, tornadoes, floods, and wildfires across the nation. During and after natural disasters, denominationally funded regional organizations offer relief by providing shelter, water, and hospital care, but the emotional, psychological, and spiritual care components are left with local clergy. How do trauma-trained clergy respond? As you will see by the following story, new congregational and community challenges require new skills.

THE VALLEY CAUGHT FIRE

In 2020, as the Covid-19 pandemic was well underway in the United States, psychologists measuring stress among people in all age categories documented increasingly high rates. People had little personal control, were misinformed, and faced uncertainty. Every step outdoors was fraught with interpersonal anxiety. The economy was threatened, and millions of people lost their jobs, businesses, and homes. And then fires and hurricanes left half a million people in Texas, California, Oregon, and Washington State under evacuation orders and facing what was called a "compound hazard risk."[1]

Our southern Oregon mountain valley is dotted with small towns and surrounded by mountains on all sides. During the first summer of Covid-19, locals cherished the clean air and spent time outside safely enjoying family and friends even as more people were hospitalized and dying. In September, a second trauma befell us. A massive fire erupted, driven by increasingly frequent hot winds. Someone in our town of Ashland set a fire to cover up either a murder or his own suicide. The burning body set Ashland and two smaller towns to the northwest—Talent and Phoenix—ablaze.

I was out in the driveway late that morning, raking leaves that gusty winds lifted and swirled in all directions. Here in the tinder-dry west, we have learned to fear such winds. An hour later, multiple fires exploded. Chaotic winds shifted into residential neighborhoods and stoked fires along a walking/biking path near a creek, creating a wind tunnel for the fire to use. From there it passed through backyards, and up hillsides. Flames consumed twenty mobile home parks, an assisted living center, a bank, an entire strip mall, and a third-generation family donut shop. The fire's heat was so intense that everything it touched turned to dust. The fire moved in such random fashion that fire crews were overwhelmed. In one neighborhood the water hydrants ran dry. In another, the emergency alert system was never activated.

Good Samaritans ran through neighborhoods knocking on doors, organizing hose brigades, and escorting people with walkers and wheelchairs. One man lost his life when he stayed behind to help others. People ran from their homes carrying their pets and nothing else. People who had left for the grocery store an hour earlier could not get back to their homes in time to save anything at all. A police officer escorted one elderly woman to her home and told her she had just five minutes to grab things. She opened the door and stood in the living room—hearing crackling fires and sirens all around her—and froze in place, unable to collect her thoughts or her belongings.

In just a few hours, blocks of businesses for twenty miles were pulverized, and 2,500 people fled their homes and apartments. Many displaced residents who camped out in their cars amid the smoke to avoid Covid-19 in the shelter, eventually learned that their residences had burnt to the ground. Overwhelming fear filled our three closely connected small towns and would remain there during the following weeks and months. While each person's trauma load was different depending on various circumstances, everyone in multiple fire areas ended up with it. One million acres across Oregon state were burning that September, with five hundred thousand people, including residents of rural areas and suburban Portland, under evacuation orders.[2]

No place seemed safe for those of us in the valley during the fires. Evacuation orders are traumatizing in and of themselves. Trapped by fires all around us, we loaded up our car, checked on neighbors, and awaited instructions. Although we were prepared to leave, evacuation plans were chaotic because all major highways were blocked off for emergency vehicles or closed due to spot fires. Truck drivers on the freeway who consulted Google Maps exited just north of the fire, and by doing that, they blocked evacuation routes through the burning towns. Absurdly, television stations aired Dr. Oz and Ellen as if nothing were happening.

For weeks, our air hung thick with the residue of burned trees and blackberry vines and red dust from chemical fire retardants. Unavoidable toxic air and prolonged exposures scarred the lungs of those who worked outside, lived in tents, or stayed overnight in their cars to avoid sheltering with others. Think about breathing the vapors of everything stored in your basement or garage. All in one whiff, you breathe in old paints and varnishes, rat poison, antifreeze. Then imagine what a house exudes as it burns: benzine from plastic pipes, refrigerant, asbestos siding, lead. Our air was the worst in the world for nearly three weeks.

At our house, we focused on controlling what little we could. We had an allergy filter in our heating and air conditioning unit and a HEPA filter in the bedroom that blinked red constantly. We stopped cooking on our gas range to lower the toxic load. On the rare occasions when we had to go out, we wore heavy masks and quickly came back in.

For over a month, the air smelled foul, leaving us with a visceral sense that the world was ending. Satellite pictures of the planet at that time showed brown dust swirling above massive fires across the western states and captured an endangered earth looking nearly extinct.

My husband and I were among "the lucky ones"; our home was safe because the wind shifted northward and away from our neighborhood. We were spared the intense trauma load that many others experienced after seeing their yards or homes in flames, racing away in cars or on foot, unsure they would come out alive. But as we listened to the stories of many victims, we caught their trauma vicariously. We too had ongoing traumatic stress responses.

What's Going on Here?

After natural disasters, trauma can move through communities leaving primary and secondary trauma. Anyone who has lived near a raging wildfire carries emotional reactivity when winds grow hot or emergency alerts ring. The loss of a safe place to live is devastating, and thick smoke intensifies physical and psychological stress. People feel trapped, and cortisol races through their bodies. Their brains become frantically scrambled. They feel powerless to protect themselves.

Multiple threats increase trauma and make recovery more challenging. After the fires in our valley had been put out, people described trauma symptoms of various types and degrees: increased social isolation, distressing memories, hypervigilance, negative moods, avoidance, irritability, nightmares, and intrusive dreams. Every time the wind picked up, people became anxious. Would the embers erupt into fires again? An eerie pall covered the area for several months, literally and emotionally. Reporters, who were traumatized too, described the burned areas using apocalyptic language.

Tender Touch

Here's an exercise to help you lower your physiological responses to these stories about trauma during natural disasters. When you begin to feel anxious or notice physical discomfort, you can calm your nervous system with a gentle touch. Perhaps hold one hand tenderly in the other or place your hands on your cheeks or belly—avoiding any place where you have experienced unwanted touch. Put your hands over your heart and pat your heart the way you might pat a baby. This touch calms and redirects energy in the central nervous system. Give yourself tender touch while you are sitting with others, particularly hearing traumatic stories.

CLERGY ON THE FRONT LINES

A local pastor and respected colleague who had taken time off and gone to the Pacific coast before the fire broke out waited anxiously in exile after learning that his neighborhood was evacuated. Once residents were allowed to return, he and his wife drove through the devastation, looking at piles of metal that were once cars and chimneys protruding from rubble, not knowing whether their house would be there. It was. A pastor at heart, he quickly turned his focus toward helping the roughly dozen families in his parish whose homes were destroyed.

A week after the fire, during the initial phases of response and recovery, he called me and said, "Can you help the clergy in the valley? We're overwhelmed by all this trauma." He was traumatized himself, not because he was weak or "couldn't handle it," but because it took great courage to support people at the evacuation center, the hotel parking lot, and the food and clothing distribution centers. He had stepped into highly emotional territory, where people were constantly in distress, their central nervous systems in overdrive, in fight, flight, and freeze responses.

Victims/survivors in fire zones and faith leaders helping them had to make rapid and supposedly rational decisions while their cognitive abilities were clouded by the trauma. Total strangers turned to my colleague and other clergy in the valley for help, trusting them simply because they were clergy. As trauma victims/survivors spilled out their stories—or went deeply into avoidance and became numb—clergy throughout the area observed, listened, and caught their trauma. They were honored to help, but they also became acutely aware that they were ill-prepared, working by instinct and intuition and hoping and praying that they were offering more help than harm. My colleague said he wanted help to feel "competent and confident" while caring for others. He was challenged by the enormity of his job and ready to become a more trauma-informed pastor.

TRAUMA CARE FOLLOWING NATURAL DISASTERS

Recovery from trauma depends on finding ongoing psychological safety—homes to live in, dependable jobs, schools for children, social support, food security, and counseling. During natural disasters such as fires, floods, hurricanes, and tornadoes, social and racial inequities are laid bare. People are statistically more likely to become jobless or have reduced work income following a disaster, but people with middle- or upper-class social status have greater access to resources during recovery than those who were living at or near the poverty threshold.[3]

These inequities became clear in our valley after the fires. Driving up the highway through the devastation, we could see that some shopping centers and newer homes had been defended while unchecked flames devastated mobile home parks nearby. A newly retired man who used every penny in his savings account to purchase a manufactured home with cash in August watched it being destroyed by fires in September and said through his tears, "I just didn't have the money to insure it."

Mobile park residents were typically seniors or multigenerational Black, Brown, Indigenous, and immigrant families. Migrant farm workers, landscapers, retail sales workers, home health aides, restaurant servers, and fry cooks were left in financial limbo without a way to restart their lives. In one of our valley's school districts, 85 percent of enrolled children and many of their teachers were homeless after the fire.

Resident Beatriz Gomez, age forty-one, said, "They wiped out the poor. . . . They wiped out the Mexicans." Searching through debris, her brother Jairo Gomez found a metal bracelet with his name on it that he had kept since he came to the United States from Oaxaca, Mexico. He searched through the ashes for a coin collection belonging to his ten-year-old son who, he said had been crying every night. "I'm an immigrant, I came here with nothing to this country. I know what it's like to have nothing and start over," Mr. Gomez said, "but they [my children] don't."[4]

Six months after the fire, roughly five hundred families were still living in hotel rooms due to the shortage of affordable housing—a situation that had existed for years that was exacerbated by the fire's destruction of additional homes. Hard-hit mobile home communities and apartment buildings took longer to rebuild than private homes, and some mobile park owners established new space rental rates, pricing out previous occupants. A California developer hired a cleanup crew from Florida to speed the process along. The company violated asbestos removal requirements, polluting the area near remaining residents. Many homeowners would never rebuild due to the maze of local, state, and federal regulations or inadequate insurance reimbursements. Meanwhile, prolonged stays in motel rooms eroded victims' mental health.

Financial help was not available to everyone. The Federal Office of Emergency Management (FEMA) rejected more than half of fire victims' applications, many due to forms filled out incorrectly or a lack of documents (which had burned up in the fires!). It took a year for approved recipients' FEMA mobile housing to arrive. FEMA didn't help people with work or student visas and is never available to migrant farm laborers. According to reporter April Ehrlich, who was also evacuated during the fire, FEMA denied fourteen thousand requests by fire victims in Oregon.

FEMA denial rates after other disasters are similarly high; 60 percent of applicants in Puerto Rico (following Hurricane Maria) and one quarter in Texas (following Hurricane Harvey) were denied. Sadly, people with higher incomes are more likely to receive assistance than those with lower incomes.[5] In contrast, affluent residents and business owners with more resources and more social standing start over again more quickly. People with adequate insurance, family support, close friends, and faith communities typically recover fully and have less risk of developing PTSD.

Social support for people in all class and ethnic groups can mitigate against trauma effects, and faith communities play a powerful role in providing emotional and logistical support and other safety nets that enhance healing. Clergy providing trauma-informed care look for ways to form helpful community and governmental partnerships to make sure that people are treated ethically and know how to access available resources.[6]

Starting Places

While helping fire victims, our clergy learned that the question "Who is my neighbor?" needs to be followed by another: *"What trauma has my neighbor endured?"* Clergy first responders in our valley learned to address the psychospiritual needs of the fire victims they were helping. Their plan included the following elements:

1. Starting with the present trauma, clergy carefully listened to victims' accounts of past trauma experiences to avoid topics or situations that could be retriggering, possibly impeding or delaying recovery.
2. Letting go of assumptions about the recovery process and using open-ended questions, they avoided trying to "fix" anyone.
3. Clergy invited people to tell their stories at their own pace and in their own time, never probing or rushing the process.
4. Knowing that memory loss and confusion are typical trauma symptoms, they believed victims' stories, even when details were missing, vague, or scrambled.
5. They maximized safety and built trust by letting victims know that their stories would not be repeated without their permission, and they maintained professional boundaries.
6. They invited victims to talk about their spiritual needs without proselytizing and connected them to appropriate spiritual or faith-based leaders and communities.

AVOIDING HARM

Unfamiliar with the complex way traumatic memory works, faith leaders can increase the likelihood of posttraumatic stress disorder (PTSD) after natural disasters through missteps during victim interviews. Researchers who studied interviews with 9/11 trauma victims gained new insights. In the first few weeks after their traumas, survivors who were questioned about what specifically happened to them were more likely to have lasting symptoms—such as flashbacks, intrusive memories, and increased physiological arousal—than those who were not debriefed. The problem was twofold. First, by evoking concrete details within the trauma, these memories became more rather than less vivid and frightening. Second, those memories were seared into the visual cortex rather than left to dissolve and dissipate.

How this process works is somewhat akin to what happens when a bright light is shone into your eyes and then withdrawn. You continue to "see" the light for some time afterward, the intensity gradually reducing until the light is finally no longer there. Visualized trauma can dissipate similarly over time. But being asked to recall it would be like someone shining a light into your eyes again to see if the first one had disappeared. Trauma-informed therapists no longer probe their clients for details about frightening experiences. They don't shy away from victims or send "don't talk" messages; they simply allow the victim to set the pace and talk or keep silent about all they have endured.

I believe that victims know instinctively how to heal and when to tell their stories. Some trauma survivors don't talk about what happened to them until months or years later, and yet they fare better overall than the individuals who are debriefed within a short period of time.

Precisely because clergy are trusted and capable listeners, people are likely to pour out their hearts to them. Trauma survivors may also be inclined to override their own needs for privacy if asked to do so by clergy. Clergy need to avoid questions that overtly or even subtly coerce trauma storytelling. They need to do so, not in avoidance or by projecting their fear about hearing the story, but with an attitude of openness and even caution that says, "You may want to talk about the details of what happened on down the road, but that's not necessary and may not be helpful for you just now." Or they might say, "I'm not a trauma-informed therapist, so you may want to talk about details that could reawaken your trauma with someone I can refer you to."[7]

Victims of trauma know what it is like to feel powerless, and so it is essential that helpers let victims be in charge not only about decisions but about storytelling too. Sometimes the need to hear the victim's whole story is our ego's vicarious "need" to share suffering or is due to survivor's guilt. We need to catch this response and address it during supervision or in our own therapy. We need to have the wisdom to know when we are, proverbially speaking, in over our heads in order to protect the people we serve.

SOCIAL JUSTICE AND TRAUMA HEALING

With natural disaster trauma a growing reality in the United States—from flooded farmlands and towns along rivers, to ocean coastline communities under water, to western states ablaze with tinder-dry forests—clergy first responders can implement individual healing strategies such as the ones above, but we have another role to play. Facing the social injustices laid bare in each natural disaster, we cannot alleviate community trauma without addressing the economic, class, race, gender, and ethnic barriers to safe housing and social services before, during, and after disasters. Clergy are in a good position from which to preach about these injustices and work alongside social service agencies. Joining recovery teams, writing letters to newspapers, posting blogs, and agitating for change are necessary for the healing of community-wide trauma. As we come alongside victims, will we allow ourselves to be motivated and changed by what we see?

After the wildfires here in the west, clergy responders became curious about why some individuals responded with resilience and others changed for the worse. The answer clearly depended on prior traumatic experiences within the lifespan of each individual and how they had been able to address those. Victim resiliency depended on social and economic status, retraumatization from systemic racial bias, and transgenerational precursors. To help someone with trauma, we have to know their history. We have to meet with parishioners or community members right where they are, without presumptions, and be aware of the social barriers or advantages they face.

Social equity awareness must be included in every recovery plan and in every provision of help and care. According to a Substance Abuse and Mental Health Services Administration (SAMHSA) report, "People in the United States and around the world who are of low SES [socioeconomic status] are more likely to live in housing that is vulnerable to disasters." They live in more substandard housing, and they lack transportation. Many Black, Indigenous, and people of color (BIPOC) face language barriers and racial discrimination. A natural disaster reduces their SES, exacerbating stress and leading to poorer mental health outcomes. The report continues, "Because people of low SES have fewer assets, they have less to lose, and when they experience financial loss in disasters, a given amount of loss has a greater financial impact on them than it will on people of higher SES, as the loss is proportionally greater."[8]

A long-term study after Hurricane Katrina showed higher levels of posttraumatic stress, psychological distress, and health complaints among those with social and economic disadvantages, with symptoms lasting four and even eleven years after the disaster. The longer it took for people to find housing and medical care and to reestablish social networks, the greater their stress became. The study showed that "low-income people and members of racial/ethnic minority groups (were) more likely to live in disaster-prone areas and in lower-quality housing." Among these groups, the trauma of property loss was minimal compared to the ill effects of "bereavement, fear for one's life, and uncertainty about the safety of loved ones."[9]

Disaster victims who can't find safe and adequate permanent housing after initial sheltering assistance runs out have prolonged traumatic symptoms and greater mental and physical health declines. They are more likely to have depression and experience distress. Their traumatic stress takes longer to heal, making another roadblock to their future climb out of poverty or into a better SES. Studies after disasters across the nation clearly point to socioeconomic status as a key indicator for poor mental health outcomes, including acute trauma and PTSD. In climate-related disasters, the prophetic call to look after the poor and the widow must be loud and persistent. Trauma-informed care is consistent with Jesus's call to tend to the needs of "the least of these"[10] by upending old patterns of power and privilege and, in essence, placing people who typically end up last, first.

FAITH COMMUNITIES RESPOND

During and after disasters, trauma-informed clergy promote healing for members and friends in their faith communities and reach out to underresourced people. Congregations offer individual and family support to those most affected, especially people who are ineligible for government assistance or fall through the cracks due to inadequate mental health support.

Clergy offering best practices within the ethic of "do no harm" examine their internalized gender, race, and class biases along the way. This work leads them to the second undertaking—getting involved at city, state, and federal levels to advocate for equitable treatment and recovery plans that give survivors a chance to start over with improved social status.

In our community, clergy participated in weekly support groups for survivors. They encouraged their congregations to adopt families in need, located extra rooms in people's homes, and found lawn spaces around town for tents. They raised money for basic needs and short-term housing. They opened their church parking lots and restrooms, rounded up RV's, and gave people somewhere to live during the rebuilding process.

Many clergy in fire zones wish that they had been better prepared for a community-wide disaster. Has your faith community collaborated with local government and nonprofits to develop emergency preparedness plans? Have you met with denominational staff who respond to disasters in your area? Make it a priority to take a disaster preparedness training course in the year ahead.

Here are additional actions to take now to support present and future natural disaster trauma victims:

- Talk with your faith community about the connection between natural disasters and global climate change.
- Advocate for natural disaster mitigation in your area.
- If you are not in a natural-disaster-prone area, partner with a congregation that is vulnerable (near a coastline, on a floodplain, in an area with groundwater or drinking water contamination, or in a fire zone).
- Strengthen emergency preparedness plans and become ready to shelter people as needed.
- Reach out to representatives from your faith-based response teams and invite them to preach or speak.
- Support community programs and policies that work for social justice and climate change.

KICKING OVER A FEW TABLES

Observing beggars being taken advantage of in the marketplace around the temple, Jesus was not patient. He was not even particularly kind. He had an angry, aggressive response. He dismantled shops and turned over tables. In The Message's interpretation of Matthew 21:12–13 MSG, the story goes like this: "Jesus went straight to the Temple and threw out everyone who had set up shop, buying and selling. He kicked over the tables of loan sharks and the stalls of dove merchants." He took these actions boldly. In the very next verse it says that he had made "room for the blind and crippled to get in."

While trauma survivors try to get their feet back under them, faith communities can help them overcome prevalent roadblocks. Learning community organizing skills and practices can help congregations to expose injustice and become advocates for others during recovery. Faith communities need to stay in the recovery effort for as many months and years as it takes to rebuild homes and lives. This requires patience and perseverance.

To care for a widow in our valley, a few tables had to be turned over. Nine months after the fires, a widow who attends a local church planned to return to the mobile home park where she had lived but faced large increases in fees and new requirements. Her older single-wide mobile home had been totally destroyed, and her insurance valued the loss at $45,000. But the park developers said they would only allow new double-wide homes on their property (at around $150,000 per dwelling) and increased the monthly space rental fee substantially. The developer was featured in the local news with drawings and plans for an upscale new clubhouse and added amenities. A spokesperson was quoted, saying she was very sad that this increase shut out lower-income seniors who had been living for decades on those sites. This infuriated the homeowners and the community.

Consider how this circumstance impacted the widow's trauma recovery. How might her faith community advocate for her and other fire victims by challenging systemic social inequity? When friends and family called the corporation, their calls were not returned. It took weeks of continued public pressure by justice advocates for city officials to restrict price gouging by corporate landowners and require park managers to allow returning residents to purchase single-wide homes. Shared traumatic grief motivated clergy and congregants to become activists.

THE LARGER PICTURE

National Geographic aired the award-winning documentary series *One Strange Rock* during the lockdown year in the pandemic. My husband and I started watching it while we were locked in our home by thick, red, toxic air from fires all around us. Will Smith narrates discoveries about our incredible planet in all its glory and about its great peril. Former astronauts describe what the planet looks like from space and the way that viewpoint forever changed them. Describing the planet's awe-inspiring beauty and fragility, they offer visually stunning portraits and near-religious calls for us to protect and care for the earth.

Now that the planet's demise is evident in every natural disaster, we need to call upon everyone to change the trajectory of global warming. If we do nothing to curb climate change, more than twenty million people in the United States will become unhoused or face relocation to substandard housing in the next fifty years. More global climate disaster victims will be seeking refuge within our borders and communities. Despair could immobilize us, but action can empower us.

Climate change is not a random or fleeting problem, and saying that it is retraumatizes victims by minimizing their pain and their losses. When a woman whose family farm has been destroyed by a flood twice in ten years hears a church member tell her that it was God's will, her pain escalates. When she hears someone say that climate change is a hoax, her anger churns up like the muddy waters of the river that overflowed its banks and carved a swath through her barn and home. She fears that no one cares enough about her or her children to do something about it. Climate change denial insults people who have been devastated by winter ice storms, crop-destroying heatwaves, tornadoes, hurricanes, floods, and fires. An angry colleague quipped recently, "The fires in our area were not natural disasters; they were 'unnatural' disasters."

Prophetic preaching and congregational engagement in climate change actions give hope to these disaster victims. It's time for clergy to fully validate disaster victims' experiences by preaching about ways to reverse our current national and global course. Natural disasters are not signs that the end is near, even though they feel that way. They are signs that the end could be near if we continue to believe a human dominion narrative that exploits the earth and all that lives upon it.

CHAPTER SEVEN

RESPONDING TO RACIAL VIOLENCE
CLERGY, CONGREGATION, AND COMMUNITY ENGAGEMENT

Mighty deliverer, free us from our bondage to distinction, privilege, and caste. Awaken us, not with shame but with clarity, to the power in our silences and our words. When we define people as "other" or categorize them by the color of their skin, bring us up short with a moral consciousness that convicts and also liberates. May we who are preachers let ourselves be preached to and we who have power be willing to recognize our enslavement. With racialized hatred and violence standing at our doorsteps, we are all traumatized. Help us to cross over into your glorious promised land, where sin and hatred have no purchase and people are no longer bought, sold, or killed. Amen.

Throughout US history, people have experienced and witnessed racial trauma. Employing denial and victim blaming, the very real toll trauma takes on individuals, families, and societies has been minimized and ignored. But a pivotal moment took place at the corner of Chicago Avenue and Thirty-Eighth Street in Minneapolis on May 25, 2020, when a courageous teen named Darnella Frazier took out her cellphone and filmed the killing of George Floyd by a White police officer. The nine minutes it took for Derek Chauvin's knee to close off Floyd's airway prompted a reckoning with the truth about societal trauma and racial violence. For some Christians, and many progressive clergy, this image is nearly as powerful as the cross upon which Jesus's suffering demanded an end to violence. Nine months later, a violent uprising in our nation's capital by self-avowed members of White supremacist groups added to the urgency clergy felt about renewed study, compassion, and action. They asked, "What religiously sanctioned themes have supported racial violence toward Black people and the Black community?" and "What do I need to do in response to these polarizing times?"

I will look at our national legacy of racial violence toward Indigenous people, immigrants, and other racially harassed and traumatized groups in a future chapter. For now, I want you to look specifically at Black trauma and White trauma and ways that they overlap and escalate violence.

My goal is that you learn (and help your congregants learn) ways to respond when White-on-Black violence erupts on the news or, as it did in my town, in the back parking lot at a local hotel. Whether you are serving in a city, suburb, or small town, this awakening in history offers an opportunity for compassion and change. It offers insights about pastoral care for trauma victims, and it calls us all to do more than watch from afar. As you read, I will be asking you to explore your own racism, come alongside those who experience trauma from racial violence, and work for justice to change entrenched attitudes and social systems that retraumatize Black individuals and families.

~

"Steal away, steal away, steal away to Jesus. Steal away, steal away home, I ain't got long to stay here." These words and the traditional melody that accompanies them are attributed to Wallace Willis, a slave of a Choctaw freedman in what history books call the "Indian Territory,"[1] and were written before the Emancipation Proclamation of 1863. He passed it along by singing it within earshot of Rev. Alexander Reid, a minister at a Choctaw boarding school. Reid was so moved by the song that he transcribed the words and melody and then sent it to the Jubilee Singers, a choir of former slaves receiving their education at Fisk University in Nashville. Their powerful public performances led to the song's inclusion in many hymnals still today.[2]

I learned to sing "Steal Away" while sitting in a church pew in an all-White Protestant congregation. I thought it was a song about death and eternal peace with God. White preachers had whitewashed its meaning. Its evocative melody and lyrics would have been heard much differently by American descendants of slavery (ADOS).

I grew to love the song as a child. Years later when I was a hospital chaplain, I found myself singing it at the bedside of a frail silver-haired woman in her late nineties. She was dying and her breath was very labored. Each in breath was painful for her and for those of us witnessing her last hours. The staff felt relief that a minister had come to "do something." I sat down at her bedside, slipped my pale hand beneath her limp dark one, and timed my breathing to hers. Then I said a prayer and this hymn emerged. I softly began singing, "Steal away, steal away, steal away to Jesus." Her body calmed.

My bishop at the time, Leontine T. C. Kelly, was a powerful preacher of the African American folk church style. I was at a large conference meeting where she proclaimed the hope she had found in Jesus's resurrection. "I'm not afraid of dying," she said. "I know who owns the property on both sides of the river." I borrowed Bishop Kelly's faith as I kept on singing, "Steal away. . . ." I didn't know all the verses, but I'm pretty sure by a slight smile on the woman's cracked lips that she did. And while I was offering it as a prayer that her journey across that river be full of peace and even anticipated joy, the song may have held an even deeper meaning for her.

This song is one among many coded songs that were used to relay messages from slave to slave along the Underground Railroad. Facing daily traumatic violence, Willis and other slaves created lyrics with double meanings, including "Wade in the Water," which described places to meet Moses for the exodus north, and "Sweet Chariot," which promised liberation when the chariot swings low into the Deep South. While White slave owners preached a gospel that sanctioned slavery, "The slaves in turn memorized portions they felt were beneficial for them and rejected others that they felt were not."[3]

Coded slave songs described freedom and liberation within the exodus narrative. The Fisk Jubilee Singers who helped popularize the hymn would have understood these coded messages and secret meanings.[4] "Steal away" might have meant "Escape from here, now is the time. The master is trembling, and you can escape." The song's message was not just eternal; it was grounded in a vision of freedom from the overseer's whip and the master's violence. "Freedom rings within my soul"—I won't be in bondage much longer. More than 150 years later, Black people in America are regularly denied their freedoms and violently punished for demanding them. My next story sadly illustrates this point.

> *Please take note that the following section in this chapter may reawaken trauma symptoms for anyone who has experienced racial violence or loved someone who has been killed. If you continue reading, please be aware of your emotional and physical responses to the material and quit at any time. Whether you identify as BIPOC or White, your racial trauma may arise as you think about and learn more about ways to respond.*

THE MURDER OF AIDAN ELLISON

Local newspapers reported that a man had been shot and killed in his car in a hotel parking lot a mile from my home at around 4:00 a.m. on November 23, 2020, following an argument. This is a quiet town where just three murders have occurred in the past twelve years. As the press reported the situation with very few details, rumors flew, with most people in our community assuming this was a drug deal gone wrong.

The victim, Aidan Ellison, was a nineteen-year-old graduate from our local high school. He had lost his job when devastating fires a few months before destroyed the business he had worked for, and he was staying with another evacuee at the hotel. In the middle of the night, she gave him the keys to her car so he could have some time to himself. Aidan Ellison was sitting in the parking lot, playing music while Black.

A forty-seven-year-old White man named Robert Paul Keegan came out of another hotel room and approached the car. Due to a pending trial, there is no detailed public record of exactly what happened next. It was reported in the news that the hotel's night clerk heard a verbal altercation and went out back, and then soon returned to the lobby. Perhaps he was thinking the situation had been resolved. If so, he was tragically wrong. Keegan returned to the hotel room—where he had been staying with his third-grade son since their home was destroyed in the fires—to get his unregistered gun. He then went back out to the parking lot and shot Aidan at point blank range. Aidan died instantly.

Precious Edmonds, spokesperson for the Southern Oregon Black Leaders, Activists, and Community Coalition, said the killing itself, as well as the way it was framed by police and local media outlets, is an example of the area's racial history and present bias: "To be clear, Aidan was murdered because he was a young Black person who made a white man uncomfortable and refused to submit to that man's personally-perceived authority—not because he was listening to music too loudly."[5]

Local media outlets initially attempted to somewhat absolve Keegan by reporting that he was a victim of the fires and recounting his work as a school volunteer. People raised money for his defense, which added more pain for Aidan's family and further fractured the community. Three days later, however, the police chief, Tighe O'Meara, posted on Facebook, "It has been reported in some local media sources that I said this murder was 'because of' something. The only thing that caused this murder was the suspect's actions, 100 percent. It is completely immaterial what led up to it." Edmonds noted, "He was listening to his music too loudly—that's irrelevant, it doesn't change a thing, how good the man who shot him was. All of those things are not relevant to what occurred. But that's the narrative, that's the frame of white supremacy."[6]

This local tragedy, along with the murder of George Floyd six months earlier, awakened people in our community to ingrained assumptions about White identity and to the pervasive presence of racial violence. We who serve as clergy in this valley could no longer imagine that these issues are challenges only for Black pastors in big cities where anti-Black and other race-directed violence is more commonplace. We had to ask hard questions about that night and challenge ourselves to get uncomfortable, to learn, and to become antiracist leaders.

Here are key questions clergy asked:

- How does racial bias get in our way as we plan personal, congregational, and community-wide responses?
- How do we initiate (or expand) conversations about the racism in our predominantly White-identified community?[7]
- How do we challenge our community's skewed narrative that we live in a place where everyone is open to diversity and all strangers are welcomed?
- How can we repair the exclusionary and violent racist history in our county and state?

Writing about Aidan's death, I find myself wanting to understand Keegan's White rage and violence, and I am simultaneously repulsed by my curiosity. In the lynching years in US history, White people were invited to come and watch the mutilation and killing of Black people—even to take home body parts or pictures as souvenirs. I do not want to be a witness like that! But I can no longer minimize or deny this violence. As a trauma-informed pastor in a small town, I am called to learn all I can about racism (starting with my own) and White-bodied supremacy so that I am better equipped to respond to victims with an open heart and mind and to avoid retraumatizing them out of unconscious racial bias or ignorance. In order to dig more deeply into racial trauma, let's turn now to experts in the field.

What's Going on Here?

Resmaa Menakem, in his book *My Grandmother's Hands*, explains that racial trauma is an inherited condition that is carried in both White and Black bodies. He calls this White-bodied trauma and Black-bodied trauma: "Many African Americans know trauma intimately–from their own nervous systems, from the experiences of people they love, and, most often, from both."[8] Black bodies carry historical pain. White masters, seeking wealth and status through the slave trade, tore people from their homes, locked them in slave ships, and forced them to endure physical and mental violence on plantations. The Emancipation Proclamation promised a better future that never materialized, leading to Jim Crow violence and lynching. Black bodies have been assaulted, murdered, raped, shot at, whipped, brutalized, and killed in America by White people for hundreds of years. Their lives have repeatedly been torn apart as family members have been incarcerated. They are watching as their children are gunned down by the police.

The American experience for many Black individuals and families is repeatedly traumatic. Ongoing and persistent trauma leads to acute stress disorder and chronic PTSD. Psychologists identify racial trauma and race-based stress as conditions that share symptoms with PTSD but are uniquely different, based on real or perceived racial discrimination. Menakem notes that "these include threats of harm and injury, humiliating and shaming events, and witnessing harm."[9] Threats to integrity and personal well-being happen frequently for many Black individuals. Black trauma is reawakened by news reports about yet another racially motivated killing, too often justified by pervasive victim-blaming.

INGRAINED FEAR

The majority White culture in the United States still perpetuates a predominant myth about Black men in particular and the Black body in general. Black bodies are seen as "dangerous and threatening . . . impervious to pain . . . [needing to be] managed and controlled by any means necessary."[10] Kelly Brown Douglas adds sexuality to discourse about Black-bodied trauma. She notes that slave owners justified their predatory sexual violence by placing blame elsewhere. Claiming that Black slaves were hypersexual and likely to violate their White wives and daughters, slave owners deflected shame from their own sexual violence, including their ownership and rape of slaves.[11] Historian Ayumu Kaneko writes that the Black rapist myth has long been used to "justify the disenfranchisement of African-American citizens; to terrorize and drive a dividing wedge into the solidarity of the Black community; to elevate white women onto the pedestal of 'White chastity and purity," thereby continuing them within the regime of white patriarchal supremacy; and to undermine interracially cooperative political and social movements."[12]

Justifications for racial violence began over four hundred years ago when slavery was instituted in the Americas, and they continue to the present day. Aidan's murder in a local hotel parking lot and other White-on-Black killings expose this history. The myth that Black men are all criminals and drug addicts fed into our community's first assumptions about what happened in the parking lot that night. The myth of the massively strong "Black Brute" was used by defense attorneys in Officer Chauvin's trial for the murder of George Floyd. As long as these myths prevail, trauma will be their historic legacy.

~

Discourse about Black men and mythologies about them have influenced many generations, including yours and mine. It is essential that we learn about and change racialized trauma reactions in order to respond to community violence and care for victims and their families. The hardest part of this journey is a deep dive into racism.[13]

As a White person, it's my job to look at when, where, and how I was raised with, absorbed, and perpetuated racist ideas. Along with too many White Americans across hundreds of years, I was raised to be afraid of Black people. In my childhood, racial fear was planted in my central nervous system when my parents drove through areas in Columbus, Ohio, where Black people lived, and my father told us kids in the back seat to lock our car doors. White supremacy was on full display in our suburb, where it was illegal for any property owner to rent to or sell to people other than Whites. Mother taught me that I could be friendly to the kind maid from "downtown" (a term that meant "where the Blacks live") when she came to our home every other week, but I could not ask her questions about her life or linger with her more than a few minutes after my "hello." Walking home after middle school, I saw a dozen Black maids standing at bus stops near my house nearly every day. By age fourteen, I had already learned to avoid eye contact and walk on the other side of the street. Racial fear was already lodged in my nervous system.

To this day, I have irrational surges in cortisol when I am alone in an elevator with a Black man or when driving through a "downtown" in any city. When my body reacts to a perceived threat, especially one that *does not exist*, it is my job to notice and deal with these physical responses and to gracefully interpret them as misplaced and ancient fears. I also have to calm down my central nervous system through deep breathing and other mindfulness practices. These rushes of fight/flight/freeze in my body are old, embedded responses.

Menakem explains it this way: "A different but equally real form of racialized trauma lives in the bodies of most white Americans."[14] He names the pain inside the White person who commits White-on-Black violence as unhealed—"dirty"—pain: "When someone with unhealed trauma chooses dirty pain (avoided or repressed pain) over clean pain (acknowledged and healed pain), the person may try to soothe his or her trauma by blowing it through another person—using violence, rage, coercion, deception, betrayal, or emotional abuse."[15] Sometimes a trauma victim's rage turns inward to avoid confrontations, leading to self-destructive behavior.

As a psychologist, I feel compelled to ask, "On the day that Aidan was killed, what was going on inside Keegan?" Did he have "unclean" trauma coursing through his body? Why did he have so little control over his own rage? Was he coping with his trauma after the loss of his home (or adding to it) with alcohol and medications, or was he following extremist hate groups on the web that exacerbated his powerless feelings? These questions do not justify his actions; they do direct us to understanding and stopping White violence.

In what ways has the community I live in contributed to Keegan's belief that he had a right to control Aidan, and how can we talk together about White violence? Playwright Lorraine Hansberry said in 1964, "We have to find some way with these dialogues to show and encourage the white liberal to stop being a liberal and become an American radical. . . . The basic fabric of our society, after all, is the thing which must be changed to really solve the problem."[16] How has community-wide denial about racial harassment and violence in our area contributed to the problem?

Before you read more, take a moment to check in with your body. Tackling the subject of racialized violence requires that you pay attention to even small shifts in your cortisol and adrenalin. Working on racism inevitably means that you will feel arousal in your sympathetic nervous system. You may feel it as distress, anger, fear, or sadness. Here's a way to counter that experience and increase your sense of calm before reading on:

> ### Belly Breathing
> *Your breathing pattern can control your nervous system. Inhaling activates the sympathetic fight/flight/freeze response. Exhaling is linked to the parasympathetic nervous system, which reverses the body's alarm system. If your diaphragm is constricted, your breath will be shallow and up in your chest, which makes your entire body tense. To correct this, take a few deep breaths and breathe into your belly. Imagine your belly expanding all the way to the bottom of your torso. Do this as many times as you need to until your mind is quiet and calm.*

ENDING WHITE VIOLENCE

How do we describe the physiological arousal in the bodies of murderers and mass shooters? Do we call it hate? Or pain? Or fear? How can we disrupt it when it is based in dominance and projected shame? Whenever the bodies of BIPOC people are demonized as hypersexual, dangerous, and seductive, violence is legitimized. Aidan's killer seems to have felt he had the right to control Aidan based on the color of his skin.

Will our community be changed by Aidan's death? The answer depends on our willingness to value Aidan's life *and* challenge macro- and microaggressions that are experienced daily by Black, Brown, and Indigenous people in our area. Aidan was a young, talented Black man with a full life cut short. As his family and friends continue to experience traumatic grief, how will we keep his memory alive and use his death as a call to action? How will Minneapolis keep George Floyd's memory alive? How will people in Louisville, Kentucky, honor Breonna Taylor's life and change the circumstances that led to her death? Victims of racial violence whose names we never hear, in places we'd least expect to be dangerous places for people of color in America, also deserve our grief and cries for justice.

As I will say often in this book, we have to listen to the wisdom of victims and survivors. The fear within Aidan seconds before he so tragically died is now carried in his mother, his younger siblings, and the community. Black children who witness violence carry fear, and they will likely carry it forward to their children. When a police officer knocked on the door of a Black household this month, an unidentified neighbor said she overheard the children yelling, "Don't kill our dad!"

EXPOSURE TO TRAUMA

As a White person watching a Black man's murder on replayed videos, I become sad and weary and, honestly, ashamed. For a Black person watching, intense anger from repeated experiences with violent death at the hands of White people (especially White police officers) can evoke a fight/flight/freeze response. As Black people watched George Floyd's murder, they transformed the energy of fear into strength to resist, protest, and fight back, proclaiming, "That's it, we've had enough, this is too many."

The diagnostic manual in psychiatry claims that trauma definitions do not apply when people are exposed to the aversive details of traumatic events through television or social media. I respectfully disagree. The videotaped recording of Floyd's murder awakened rage to the point where over half a million protestors in the United States took to the streets, joined by people in over sixty countries.[17] Partially motivated by their retraumatization, people risked Covid-19 infection to meet violence with moral force.

Watching this killing moved people to action because it triggered people's physical, psychological, and spiritual trauma memories. People who have had guns pointed at them or have had sons die from drug overdoses or suicides and sexual and physical assault survivors, who intimately know the hatred that a shooter's face communicates, were all retraumatized. They felt adrenalin rushing through their bodies, their cortisol levels rose, and they prepared for action. They took it to the streets.

Knowing about the underlying biological components within trauma motivated trauma-informed clergy to participate in community-wide responses to violence. People in our town who knew Aidan Ellison were immediately thrown into acute stress responses, but many who didn't know him were also traumatized by his killing. Retriggered trauma motivated them to process grief (and yes, guilt) by painting signs, waving flags, and putting their feet to the ground and their fists in the air to express their defiance against racially motivated brutality. Clergy who spoke out and marched for justice participated as allies in order to heal community trauma.

Helping a Person with Reawakened Trauma

- Reach out to people in your faith community who have previously (or repeatedly) experienced traumatic grief, gun violence trauma, and racial harassment or brutality.
- Validate their physical and emotional reactions and use the word *traumatic*.
- Ask what they need from you and from the members of your faith community.
- Offer to connect people to trauma-informed and culturally sensitive therapists.
- Know the names of supportive organizations for BIPOC people in your area, post these on your website, and hand out print copies of the list.
- Working alongside local BIPOC leaders and organizations, join community protests and speak up about the need for change.

STARTING PLACES FOR FAITH COMMUNITIES

How are you and your faith community addressing racial trauma and racial violence? If you identify as BIPOC clergy, you have shouldered the largest burden in this work for too long, and I don't expect you to do the work that Biracial- and White-identifying people must do. It is time for White people to learn more about the violence that is minimized and justified within the dominant cultural discourse and narrative.

We all need to read, reflect, and plan for change. Many congregations across the country are doing that by engaging in workshops and reading groups to learn about White privilege, White fragility, and racial violence. They have started conversations among White people about White-bodied trauma. They have reached out to BIPOC organizations to ask how to be allies for them in their work. And they have stopped expecting Black people to educate them and instead started educating themselves.

As a trauma-informed clergyperson, how can you do more? Hold a bystander/upstander training course in your congregation to equip your congregants to safely stop verbal, sexual, and racial harassment when it's observed. Ask community leaders to support policies that promote racial equity and create a social and racial equity program in your faith community. Ibram X. Kendi, in his book *How to Become an Antiracist*, notes that moral discourse and education alone will not end racial violence: "The history of racist ideas is the history of powerful policy-makers erecting racist policies out of self-interest, then producing racist ideas to defend and rationalize the inequitable effects of their policies, while everyday people consume those racist ideas, which in turn sparks ignorance and hate."[18] By engaging in public discourse and policy, clergy can be effective change makers and lead their congregations to do the same.

Preach Justice

To assist survivors of racial justice, I have suggested ways to explore your internal racism and ideas for coming alongside the victims/

survivors of racialized violence. Our next step is to use our power and privilege to create safer communities. We are called to preach about and work toward changing entrenched attitudes and social systems that retraumatize Black members in our congregations and communities.

Long after the passage of the Civil Rights Act, movement toward racial equality in the United States remains a slow and halting process. The Hartford Institute for Religious Research noted, "Eleven o'clock Sunday morning continues to be the most segregated hour in America."[19] Preaching about race relations and racial trauma in segregated congregations requires humility and courage. For preachers in our community after Aidan's death, the prophetic word included a look back in time and a call to repent and repair.

Oregon is not the only state with a deeply rooted history of racial discrimination that connects to current racial harassment. These stories need to be told. In 1859, Oregon was incorporated as a White state, the only state ever identified in this way. In 1921, our county saw the swearing in of the first Klansmen in Oregon. Bounties were offered on First Nation members.[20] Sundown laws existed here into the 1960s. This legacy has not gone away. Our town's university and regional theater are committed to equity and diversity. They bring an active BIPOC community to the area. Sadly, students and actors have been racially profiled, stalked, and verbally harassed.

Exploring Your Neighbor's Racial Trauma

What do you know about racial profiling and aggression toward BIPOC people in your community? How might you go about asking them? How does the history of racial violence in your area still affect people today? Learn more by joining a racial equity committee in your area or partner with BIPOC community members to create one.

Trauma-informed pastors look back at history and ask how racialized laws and policies still influence current racist and/or antiracist activities. When I was teaching a class to clergy about trauma care, one participant commented that the section on immigrant trauma in my book *When Trauma Wounds: Pathways to Healing and Hope* just didn't apply to the rural community in the "White church" he was serving. I did some research and found that, in fact, that clergyman is serving in a state with the second-fastest-growing number of Latinx and African immigrants in the United States. Learning this changed his mind, and coming alongside new immigrants has since become a focus in his church and in his pastoral ministry.

In spite of the evidence from multiple perspectives that racial issues affect everyone in our society, White clergy still tend to be frightened and silenced by the reactions they fear they will face from their members. I experienced pushback when I was a pastor. I preached a sermon on Martin Luther King Jr.'s birthday in a small-town church, challenging the people I served to consider their mostly White constituency while all around them the community was becoming more diverse. The following Monday, a letter went to my bishop demanding that I be reprimanded or relocated to another church for having shamed my parishioners. Unbeknownst to the letter writer, the bishop was Black, and so I remained there with encouragement.

To mollify their constituents, or quite literally to keep their jobs, too many clergy avoid calling for justice after mass shootings committed by White males, police shootings, and even during Black Lives Matter protests. Through the decades, predominately White church leaders have worsened race relations in America by asserting racial superiority and White patriarchal supremacy. In his "Letter from a Birmingham Jail" in 1963, Martin Luther King Jr. wrote, "I felt that the white ministers, priests and rabbis of the South would be some of our strongest allies." "Instead . . . too many . . . have been more cautious than courageous and have remained silent."[21] It's time for every clergyperson to preach out against the violence inflicted upon God's people in America. It will take a long overdue, unified prophetic cry for justice to counteract and heal racially inflicted trauma.

Victims need to have hope that no one else will go through the pain they have endured. Whether by joining a group for similar victims, creating nonprofit organizations, walking the streets in protest, or mounting media campaigns, victims move beyond powerlessness and become survivors by standing up and speaking out. What they need to hear from the rabbi, preacher, monk, imam, and pastor is that what was done to them was horrifically wrong.

In the aftermath of racial violence in America, preachers have often jumped too quickly to the theme of forgiveness, which retraumatizes victims by denying the depth of their pain. In 2015, when a gunman killed nine Black attendees at a prayer meeting at Emanuel African Methodist Episcopal Church in Charleston, South Carolina, among the nine victims were Sr. Pastor Clementa C. Pinckney and three other clergy. Soon thereafter, one story that preachers repeatedly told was about the congregation's incredible forgiveness. What wasn't as often mentioned was that the murderer remained unrepentant. "I would like to make it crystal clear; I do not regret what I did," Dylann Roof wrote prior to his sentencing hearing. "I am not sorry. I have not shed a tear for the innocent people I killed."[22] To justify his murderous rampage, he cited the myth I previously described, which arose during slavery—that Black men are sexual predators who endanger White women. Preaching after racially motivated killings must be done from racially informed, trauma-validating, and victim-validating perspectives. Preachers need to acknowledge that forgiveness and accountability are both faith-based responses. Mercy without justice rings hollow in survivors' ears.

Do It Anyway

As you do this work, don't expect yourself to do it perfectly. You won't be able to set aside ingrained physical and emotional responses all in one fell swoop. And you will get pushback from your congregation and community members. You may be called out on your race bias or race blindness. Place your fear in God's hands and engage in antiracist work anyway.

Once you learn all you can about your internalized racial biases, you can begin to support victims concretely. As I mentioned earlier in the book, people in our town erected a makeshift Black Lives Matter memorial along a quarter mile stretch of a walking/biking path by the railroad tracks. T-shirts with victims' names on them flapped in the wind. Within a month, vandals had stolen them all. The Black Lives Matter flag in front of the United Church of Christ was also stolen. The pastor posted a graceful note on Facebook saying that the person who had stolen the flag was helping the church contribute to Black Lives Matter through their purchase of another flag and that they would buy as many as needed. She also offered to buy one for the person who had stolen theirs. A few weeks later the flag was back up, and the memorial along the pathway had returned, one shirt and one handwritten sign at a time. A new name, Aidan Ellison, is honored among others on the fence along the path by the railroad tracks. *We pray there will be no more names.* We are healing by claiming the sacredness of each life.

In the midst of violence and racial trauma, clergy come alongside victims. Women in our town, faith leaders, and clergy gathered around Aidan's mother as she was grieving. Willing to abide in the depths of her pain, they also fought alongside her for justice when she faced discrimination in burial planning and funeral rites.

A month after Aidan's murder, I attended Zoom worship at the church where the Black Lives Matter flag had been stolen and replaced. Toward the end of her sermon, the pastor asked us to look at our bookshelves, turn the book bindings to the back if they were written by White authors, and then look at what was left. I pledged to do it, knowing that I'd have to turn the vast majority of my books around. I felt a tightness in my chest and a shame-related queasiness in my stomach at realizing the extent of my White acculturation.

Explore Your Personal Library

How many of your books are written by diverse and BIPOC authors? If you put them all together, how many shelves would they fill? Is it time to change that? Could you take up the pastor's challenge and only read books by diverse authors for the next year? Would you post and recommend a new bibliography of BIPOC authors on your webpage?

A few years ago, as I was reading Robin Diangelo's book *White Fragility*, I was urging a friend to retire in our town. She had spent her career working in the California Bay Area with frontline workers, largely from BIPOC communities. She said she was unwilling to lose the richness of a multiethnic culture. I told her I understood completely and admitted that we don't have many BIPOC people here.

I went to the post office the next day, and because I was more aware, I noticed that I was the only visibly White person in the line. This happened again in the grocery store, at an outdoor concert, and in the drugstore. I'm describing my recent experience (even though I feel embarrassed about it!) because I obviously have myopia. I am still living in my racially learned *un*consciousness. Being color blind is not a good thing; it is a numbing and avoidance strategy people use to keep from feeling internally triggered trauma.

LET THE TRAUMA TEACH US

I appreciate the work Resmaa Menakem has done to explain the trauma inside Black bodies and White bodies in America. Yesterday in another US city, one more young Black man was killed by a police officer who pulled his car over for a minor offense and then mistook her gun for her Taser. Too many more will have been killed by the time you read this. The Black Lives Matter movement has taught us many lessons, among them that confronting injustice and trauma healing go hand in hand. I recognize that becoming an antiracist and exploring racial trauma is painful, hard work, and I am sure that I am called to do it anyway. I write this believing that all clergy are called to examine racial trauma for such a time as this.[23]

～

At the National Center for Civil and Human Rights in Atlanta, I sat at a reconstructed 1960s Woolworth's Whites-only lunch counter in the museum. I hopped up onto a stool next to others with my hands on the counter and reassured myself that this was just a simulation. Through the headphones I was given, I listened to archived audio tapes of stories from participants at sit-ins. Threatening voices from angry White men behind me came through loud and clear, and I heard the cracks of Billy clubs against the countertop and felt it vibrate. I heard them shouting that I had to leave or I would be beaten.

I could not stay for the full audio presentation. My knees shook as I stood up to regain my stability. My pulse was high, my hands were sweating, and I was off balance, as if I were stepping off a boat. I searched for a steady horizon. I looked around for my husband, whose back was to me as he stood across the room looking at another exhibit. I waited for my body to settle down by taking deep, slow breaths, and I made my way over to him and slipped my hand in his.

Clearly, trauma can be triggered by a reenacted situation, even when that experience was initially someone else's and not our own. I sat down at the counter with a willingness to be made uncomfortable, trusting my soul and my body to integrate the secondary trauma it caused me. Becoming trauma-informed takes courage and a willingness to experience trauma alongside people who we think or have been told are not like us. It takes a willingness to confess our participation in racialized trauma without carrying around shame and to confront oppression and institutionalized racism within our communities and congregations. We can't afford to let any ignorance or fear prevent us from doing this work.

CHAPTER EIGHT

SECONDARY TRAUMA

CARING FOR YOURSELF AND OTHER RESPONDERS

When I am weary, gracious God, take me in your arms and comfort me. When I am burdened by shared grief, witnessed tragedy, and unspeakable suffering, give me rest. When my bones ache, my head throbs, or my back strains under the weight of human pain, lift me up. Place your healing touch on each and every trauma I carry. Teach me to know the intricate ways my body alerts me about my stress and to pay attention to my body's needs. As I care for others, be sure to remind me to care for myself as well.

Trauma-informed pastors don't shy away from people in pain. I think about Jesus's willingness to be made "unclean" by touching and interacting with people who had complex medical conditions and mental instability. Unconcerned about contagion in the way we are now, Jesus intentionally approached people in order to heal their suffering. Today, we can protect ourselves from disease as we care for people by getting immunized, wearing protective gear during hospital visits, and sanitizing and washing our hands, but our work is not risk-free. We have learned to protect our physical health, but we also need ways to protect our mental health.

Earlier in the book, I described my father's experience working with trauma-wounded veterans after World War II and the toll it took on his mental health. What he came away with from his ill-prepared work with veterans was a whole host of symptoms that were exactly like the symptoms the soldiers were experiencing. That was no coincidence. After listening for hours to the horrific details in each soldier's story, my father could not have avoided the transference.

Trauma is contagious. Clergy who provide pastoral care in fire-ravaged communities "catch" the acute stress their parishioners experience, even if they don't lose their own homes or go through the trauma of evacuation. Clergy in our area had dreams about fires, felt physically shaky when strong winds blew through their towns, had difficulty organizing sermons, were less interested in the mundane tasks of church business, and grew irritable at the seemingly petty issues their people wanted to discuss. After listening to disaster victims' stories and then walking alongside them through months of retraumatization due to red tape, FEMA denials, and homelessness, clergy became highly stressed. Some of them were taken aback by the number of secondary trauma symptoms they experienced.

Secondary Trauma Symptoms

Common symptoms that primary trauma victims experience can also be present in people who are helping them. You could experience some of these symptoms while caring for trauma victims:

- **Reexperiencing**: disturbing memories, dreams, flashbacks, and distressful ruminations *after listening to or witnessing someone else's trauma*
- **Avoidance/numbing**: avoidance of normal activities and situations, forgetfulness, diminished interests, detachment, and flattened affect *after listening to or witnessing someone else's trauma*
- **Persistent arousal**: trouble sleeping, irritability, angry outbursts, difficulty concentrating, hypervigilance, and physical reactivity to cues *after listening to or witnessing someone else's trauma*

REDUCING TRAUMA'S IMPACT

What can be done to mitigate secondary trauma? I suggest a three-step process. First, learn to recognize secondary trauma symptoms by paying attention to your cognitive, emotional, and physical responses as you care for people in your congregation and community. Second, reduce and confront old shame messages in your head: avoid telling yourself to "buck up," "push through," or any other phrase with a "should" in it. Lastly, seek out remedies and get treatment at the first sign of secondary trauma symptoms.

The first step is to recognize trauma for what it is. When you call what's going on in your body, mind, and emotions "trauma," you are less inclined to minimize and ignore symptoms. Are you using the word *exhausted* a lot when you talk to family or friends? Do you notice times when your mind seems to run off without you? Do you become irritable about minor issues? Do you find yourself ruminating about the tragic circumstances you are witnessing? Is your sleep disturbed by late-night doomscrolling on social media, unusual dreams, or early awakenings? Do you have new, frequent, or unexplained anxieties? You could be experiencing secondary trauma.

You may be inclined to ignore your symptoms because you don't want to admit to having them. What old shame-based messages from childhood could be interfering with your need for self-care? When someone was hurting in your family, what was said about that pain? Was the pain honored, or was it shamed with phrases like "What are you crying about?" or "Don't be such a . . . (put-down word)." If you grew up with these messages of rejection for feeling your pain, see if you are whispering them to yourself yet today. If the people you looked up to minimized pain by asking, "Why are you making such a big deal of it?," you may still be asking yourself that. Make a course correction if you minimize your pain or shame yourself.

In hardworking or underresourced families, parents say, "I can't take time to take care of myself, or everything will fall apart." If you grew up in such a family, did you learn to push past your own needs for rest and push yourself even harder when things went wrong? Your parents didn't know all that we now know about the brain's responses to trauma and how to heal traumatic wounds. Many of them learned to simply "armor up" and move on—their primary means for survival—which left them disconnected from their own souls and family members. If your family of origin showed you the path of denial and shame, it is time to find another path. Denial and shame will not help you heal your trauma or equip you to provide care for the people you are called to serve.

Trauma's lasting pain and secondary contagion can be reduced. Remedies include learning to manage the amount of time you spend with trauma survivors and gaining confidence to tell them when you are overloaded and need to take breaks from the stories they tell or the circumstances they are in. You can be your own firm and loving parent as you encourage yourself to eat well, rest, and take time off. Early intervention is essential.

When Emily M. D. Scott, a Lutheran pastor in Baltimore, Maryland, posted ten tips for spiritual leaders' self-care during the Covid-19 pandemic,[1] she had no idea that these simple steps would resonate with so many people. Having worked with trauma following Hurricane Sandy in New York City, she knew how hard it can be to work in times of prolonged stress. With her permission, I am sharing a slightly shortened version of her guidance. This is an excellent list for clergy serving during any type of trauma:

1. Your brain won't work as well.
    Stress messes with your sequencing, and ordering thoughts gets hard. Try one thing at a time.

2. Touch down once a day for the big picture, but focus on the tasks in front of you.
    Take in the news once a day, but the rest of the time, focus on your work to gain a sense of agency.

3. Pause to assess your gifts and your vocation and how they might meet the need in this current moment.
    Lean on the specific gifts God has given you, and take a breath before deciding how to focus your time.

4. Savor the sweet spots.
    Linger in the moments that give you comfort as long as you can.

5. Do less.
    You can do about 50 to 75 percent of what you did before the trauma. Let extra stuff fall away, and streamline what you can.

6. Sometimes, it's time for triage.
    Jump in to make something happen. It's good to move fast, but remember to move slowly afterward.

7. Adapt and pivot.
    Do it differently—take care of members and stretch outward to love your neighbors.

8. Trauma will emerge.
    You can expect past traumas and current traumas to influence your days. Notice signals your body sends you.

9. Rituals and structures of self-care are key.
    Meditate at the beginning and end of the day. Take a long walk, and have a regular talk with a dear friend.

10. You're not God.
    You don't have to rescue the whole world. We're in this together (there are people working for good in every setting) and God is still here.

When you care for traumatized people from a place of your own physical and emotional wellness, your compassion is fully available, and you can form safe and empathic relationships. If you don't have a regular therapist or spiritual director, reach out and find one to help you now or to have at the ready. During and after the pandemic, mental health care online became a viable option and made care more available wherever broadband could be accessed. Therapists representing diverse ethnicities, races, faith orientations, and genders can be found throughout the state in which you live. You don't have to be in a crisis to find one to be part of your support system. Take time to also develop collegial connections and friendships. Maintain your connections to wise family members so that if or when trauma symptoms arise, you will know what to do.

Your self-care sets an example for people in your faith community during and after community-wide traumas. When laity are called on to help others, they may expose themselves to secondary trauma: They are out in the community packing food into boxes at food banks, cleaning up after nightly shelters, greeting hospital visitors, riding along with police officers, and protesting injustice by walking down main streets. In order for faithful people to do that work, they need clergy in their worshipping communities to model self-care and to infuse them with love. They need clergy and staff who have become trauma-informed and learned to recognize secondary symptoms. They need more grace than shame when they fall apart and need to take time off or seek help for their accumulating trauma.

Pastor Julian DeShazier and leadership expert Damon A. Williams suggest that a sustainable activism by people of faith requires periods of rest from ongoing encounters with trauma, rest for which people often turn to their church. They note, "Churches are more suited than any other civic institution to offer spiritual care to the weary activists of this world. The very first churches were curated as safe spaces for the afflicted and oppressed."[2] Trauma-informed congregations provide solace and healing when it all falls apart.

HEALING PAST TRAUMATIC WOUNDS

Pastoral care will inevitably evoke your own prior primary and secondary trauma. When you sit with someone who is in great pain, your mind and body may try to protect you against harm by putting up roadblocks such as dissociating, chattering anxiously, fidgeting like a child, cutting off uncomfortable conversations, or numbing. You may unconsciously use these strategies to protect yourself from retraumatization by disconnecting from others. When people come to you after a traumatic experience, they need your empathic presence rather than your retriggered trauma symptoms. It is essential that you review your trauma history and seek treatment for intrusive symptoms.

A pastor called me to consult with him about ways to help a parishioner in distress after her father died in a war zone in Afghanistan. He met with her at his office as soon as he learned about the family's loss and then weekly for a few weeks. He felt entirely drained after each meeting: "I feel like I have to quit for the day, go home, and just sit and stare out the window for a while. I'm grumpy with my family and the church office assistant on those days too."

"And how do you feel when you are sitting across from your traumatized parishioner?" I asked.

"Well, I don't know what to say to her, so I just listen, but even that is hard. Last week I found myself stifling a yawn, which was really embarrassing, because there is nothing boring about what she's saying."

"What did you eventually say to her?" I asked.

"It's weird, but I can't even remember what I said. When she told me about the gruesomeness of his death, I just suddenly checked out."

"Where did you go?" I asked.

"I don't really know," he said.

"What did you feel in your body?"

"I can't tell you that either."

I intentionally slowed down the conversation. I took a few deep breaths and encouraged him to do the same. At that point, he could tell me what he was feeling in his body, clenched up and short of breath. After he shifted to a calmer state, we could connect his physical symptoms to his emotions, and he began to process his long-buried pain. Although he was ashamed that he couldn't offer his parishioner the empathy she needed, to his credit, after just a few of these conversations, he referred her to a trauma-informed therapist in his area. It was the best decision for them both.

What's Going on Here?

This pastor is overwhelmed by his lingering trauma symptoms from a distant experience he never thought of as traumatic. A high school friend of his enlisted and deployed to Afghanistan full of pride about serving his country after the 9/11 attacks in 2001. They had been side by side for many years in school, played on sports teams together, shared the mood swings of adolescence over late-night phone calls. The pastor was away at college when he got the call from home that his friend had died when his convoy was ambushed. To cope with his workload at school, he set aside his grief and committed himself to live a life of loving and helping others. His traumatic loss was a contributing factor in his call to ministry.

When people are ready to process traumatic experiences, a current event may link them to the past. In this case, the woman's story about her father was a link to the pastor's own loss. Even though he hadn't thought about his friend in a long while and didn't think about his loss as traumatic, it showed up in his pastoral work. His body was trying to get his attention and protect him from further exposure to similar imagery. He couldn't control what happened. He "checked out" as he was drawn into his own grief.

This is a very common experience. As a new therapist in training, I was puzzled about why I kept feeling remarkably sleepy during my sessions with one particular client. I was getting plenty of sleep, and I didn't think I was bored. It wasn't happening with other clients throughout the day. My wise supervisor taught me to recognize my fatigue and yawning as a sign of tension, not tiredness. In the same way, I told him, my dog yawns when he's tense too! Neurologically, our hindbrain (which is at the back of the skull and is also called the reptilian brain) stores physical memories and responds when we are under threat. Sometimes the threat is as great as a near death, but often it is a threat to our personal integrity or our mental health. In pastoral care, we are going to be destabilized from time to time and can work well only if we know how to listen to our symptoms and dig deeply into our own story to find the links.

SOMATIC TREATMENT MODALITIES

In the 1970s, medical biophysicist and psychologist Peter Levine[3] became curious about the way animals could experience repeated traumas (being chased by predators or fleeing fires, for example) and quickly recover. He noticed that the animals released physical energy afterward by shaking, trembling, and running. They would quite literally shake it off, which helped them return to normal. He believed that physical trauma in humans could be similarly released.

He validated this hunch by using less talk and more physical activity with patients who had PTSD. He might ask them to use movement in sessions to replicate fighting off an attack or instruct fearfully immobilized clients to jog in place in order to energize their bodies. Reawakening traumatic memory through physical reenactments, he slowly introduced patients to previously unconscious bodily experiences. When did they start trembling? When did sensations of warmth come back over them? When did their fingers get numb or tingle? This somatic (bodily) awareness helped them gradually gain power over their symptoms, and they learned calming techniques to settle down and relax. By pairing memories with stress-releasing exercises, clients built up their resilience. He helped them move through their recalled stressors rather than run or hide from them. He named this method of treatment somatic experiencing.[4] Many body-centered treatments have evolved from his work.

A dominant treatment modality using somatic memory today is eye movement desensitization and reprocessing (EMDR),[5] which focuses on moving traumatic material that was lodged in the right brain at the time of intense stress over through the hippocampus to the left brain, where it can be thought about and given story to and is less likely to emerge unbidden. EMDR therapists ask clients to describe traumatic experiences while they are feeling calm and relaxed and to stop their narratives at any point when they begin feeling anxious. At the moment of tolerance, just before the client feels overwhelmed, the therapist leads the client through a pattern of rapid lateral eye movements. Some therapists activate this side-to-side pattern using vibrating buzzers. The client holds one buzzer in each hand, and the therapist alternately activates them. This can also be done using headphones with tones that can be heard on the right, then on the left, and back again repeatedly. Whether visual, tactile, or auditory, alternative movement from the right side of the body to the left side of the body continues until the stressful recall is diminished and more tolerable. While researchers remain uncertain about the precise neurocognitive mechanism for this treatment's effectiveness, patients self-report improvement on par with other treatment modalities. This treatment has grown in popularity and is widely available. Patients with as few as ten sessions feel relief and increased mastery over symptoms.

Biofeedback is a somatic technique that helps people learn to control some of their body's overactive stress responses. In a physician's office, patients wear sensors that measure blood flow and pressure, heart rate, and muscle tension during elevated fear responses in the central nervous system and learn to activate the parasympathetic system to change them.

Some basic somatic techniques can be done without a practitioner in the room or the use of a measurement device. An increasingly popular method for calming an overactive nervous system, commonly called tapping, has become widely known and practiced. The technique, known as the Emotional Freedom Technique (EFT), can be learned and practiced in therapy, but many people learn to do it by watching online videos. Here's basically how it works: You state a strong emotion or stressful experience in one sentence and indicate the level of distress it causes you on a one-to-ten scale. You then state the problem along with an affirmation, saying something like "Even though I have this problem (or feel a strong emotion), I deeply and completely accept myself." After the statement, you tap the tips of your fingers on your body using a sequence of eight acupoints on the head and upper body and repeat the pattern until you experience little or no subjective distress.[6]

The advantages of this technique are that it can be learned easily and practiced frequently, it can be used with a variety of populations, and it is a safe and reliable way to reduce distress. In research, clinical practice, and user narratives, it has been shown to offer "profound physiological changes."[7] Tapping has been proven to calm the overactive sympathetic nervous system and reduce pernicious fight/flight/freeze responses. Like the other somatic methods I have described, tapping works from the assumption that trauma gets stuck in the undifferentiated right brain, where it is lodged as strong emotion, physical reactivity, and visual memory—all of which can be freed by moving this mass of lingering trauma across the brain through channels that were inaccessible during the fear-inducing event.

I went to a new osteopathic doctor recently to help me resolve some cranky hip pain. He'd been reading Van Der Kolk's book *The Body Keeps the Score*.[8] When he works with people, he is well aware that their perception of pain can linger long after an actual physical injury due to the connection between the body and memory. Understanding that somatization (the experiencing of mental stress physically) is common, most body workers have witnessed traumatic release during these treatments. On a massage table or during a chiropractic treatment when physical tension is released, tears often flow, anger may arise, and memories emerge. This naturally occurring process can be enhanced with intentional techniques. Among the newest somatic treatments, Tension and Trauma Releasing Exercises (TRE)[9] are a way to release physical trauma based on Levine's earlier observation that animals shake to release trauma. In these sessions (one-on-one or in groups), physical therapists help clients to over-stress muscle groups to the point of shaking and then to induce and enhance a full-bodied shaking experience. All of these methods are designed to release frozen traumatic memories and to enhance calm and well-being.

POLYVAGAL THEORY

In 1994, behavioral neuroscientist Stephen W. Porges proposed the polyvagal theory to explain physical responses before, during, and after trauma.[10] This theory led to insights for mental health practitioners and to controversy in the fields of social behavior and psychiatry. The central nervous system had for so long been understood as two distinct subsystems (the sympathetic nervous system and parasympathetic nervous system) that this theory was at first a difficult sell. When his work was published in 2011, it was considered radical because it described three complex trauma response mechanisms and shifted their source of control to the vagal nervous system.

Our bodies carry an evolutionary legacy within our nervous systems. The vagal cranial nerve is a wide and branching system throughout the body. (It gets its name from the Latin word for "wandering.") It provides a central communication hub that both stimulates and interprets what's happening in the visceral organs.

Polyvagal theory emphasizes that our oldest neurological system is the primitive dorsal vagal circuit, which protects us during trauma. It shuts down all unnecessary bodily functions to help us play dead (freeze) in response to life-threatening situations. In active shooter scenarios, for example, this function automatically awakens inside potential victims, and is sometimes lifesaving. This freeze response occurs in many animal species, thus the term "play possum" is aptly used. Polyvagal theory suggests that this primitive dorsal vagal circuit developed five hundred million years ago in the evolutionary process and that a second system (the one that has been called the sympathetic nervous system) is a mere four hundred million years old. This second system activates the fight-or-flight mechanism that helps us run, climb, or attack when we are in danger. The theory also proposes that as humans evolved, a newer system, the ventral vagal circuit, emerged just two hundred million years ago and gives us a way to promote safety and increase social engagement before, during, and after trauma.[11] These three systems work together to regulate stress, and by learning how these polyvagal states function, we can lower reactivity and prevent negative trauma outcomes.

Are we in grave danger? If so, we respond without a single thought, as I did, for example, during my automobile accident. Are we feeling okay, even when a hot-button topic is being discussed at a contentious church meeting? We are likely responding from a calm ventral vagal system wherein we feel safe and socially engaged. Stephen Porges's son Seth has described this new science in a popular podcast that illustrates these three nerve states using the analogy of a traffic light.[12]

The Ventral Vagal (Green Zone)

In this state, we are calm, our heart rate slows, digestion and saliva are stimulated, facial muscles are all active, eye contact is easy, and hearing is improved. In this state, we learn, we love, and we feel safe.

In the green zone, our face is relaxed and expressive, we understand others and listen attentively, and our body feels calm. We look rested due to good sleep and normal eating, and people can see our happiness and peace.

The Sympathetic Vagal (Yellow Zone)

In this state, we are alert to danger, and we begin to sweat as our heartbeat increases. Our pain tolerance increases, our hearing changes to extreme highs or lows, and bodily functions like cognition and digestion slow down or stop. In this state, we are less able to hear other people or sounds. Our faces may show anger and fear or become flat and unemotional.

In the yellow zone, we scan the room for escape routes, and we emotionally disconnect in order to watch out for our own safety. We can't tell what others are thinking because we aren't good at deciphering facial cues, and other people can't be sure what we are thinking either. Conversations can be misconstrued in this state, especially in cross-cultural and cross-gender communication. We may become defensive and puff ourselves up as we feel tense, and we may clench our fists and tremble.

The Dorsal Vagal (Red Zone)

In this state, we perceive extreme danger, we have completely involuntary physical responses, interpersonal signals are undecipherable to us, and the freeze system is activated (because if we get this wrong, we'll die). This is the most ancient, hindbrain response and an innocent, childlike state wherein we are totally disconnected and dependent.

In the red zone, our eyes are fixed, we may throw up or spontaneously eliminate, we feel no pain, and we breathe shallowly and slowly. We can't find words, our throat is tight, and we lose body awareness and go limp, collapse, or curl up in a ball.[13]

When we listen to our bodies, we exercise more mastery at times of stress and fear. Knowing the signs and symptoms in this traffic light analogy, we can monitor and modify changes in our reactivity. We can tell when we feel unsafe physically or emotionally in order to stop, calm down, or leave. Knowing these arousal states also helps us to see them in the faces and movements of others.

THE THEORY IN CONTEXT

I recall a time in ministry when I was the only woman at trustees and finance meetings in the parish where I served. I had the title "senior pastor" but very little earned credit and even less power. Before those meetings, I'd be in the yellow zone. I had a rapid pulse, felt shaky, and had diarrhea. My body was trying to tell me that I was scared and didn't feel safe at those meetings. Was I unsafe? No one had harmed me at those meetings, but a man in church leadership sexually harassed me during my first two years there. These leaders were his social friends who later sided with him when I finally had the courage to report my harassment and to confront the perpetrator. I didn't need to be threatened in that room. I was threatened in the *environment*, and my power and authority were doubted and maligned. My integrity was threatened, but I wasn't nearly as conscious of this as my body was. At the time, I simply thought of the experience as stressful. Had I known how to interpret my physical responses, I could have had greater compassion for myself and stopped minimizing the situation. With trauma, it doesn't matter if you have external proof of being in danger; your body offers the proof.

Now that you have a better understanding of the fight/flight/freeze system, you can offer compassion for trauma victims who ask, "Why didn't I do something?" because they were frozen during violent and dangerous experiences. Many assault victims believe that they should have escaped by running from or aggressively resisting an attacker. For centuries, courts of law and public opinion have shamed rape victims for not fighting back during their assaults and have even used their failure to exhibit bruises or lacerations as a sign they had consented. In rape cultures, victims are held responsible for their perpetrators' harm and take on the mistaken notion that they could have (or should have) been able to override their bodies' hardwired response mechanisms.

Studies have found that people overestimate their ability to stay calm when they are threatened. Women who were trained to calmly confront workplace harassers through role-playing found that in real-life confrontations with bosses or coworkers, they could not stay calm. They had expected themselves to be articulate, assertive, and competent, but they lacked sufficient information about how the body works during times of intimidation and fear.

An eye toward trauma's physiology can also help couples during conflict, who often move quickly from the calm green zone to the more reactive yellow zone, or even the disconnected and dangerous red zone. To reverse this escalation, couples establish check-in times during a conversation when they each check their pulse rate. Are either of their hearts at over one hundred beats per minute? If so, they stop the conversation until they have relaxed and returned to a state of calm before continuing. While cortisol and adrenaline were racing through their bodies, they would not have been able to hear their partner's concerns or remember them later. They would have shifted from a calm, loving, and learning interaction to a frightened, defensive, or angry position with little mental flexibility. Any two people in a challenging or conflicted conversation can use the pulse-checking technique.

How could understanding the body's reactions to threatening situations help you? If you know that an upcoming meeting will be contentious, could you use breathing and physical awareness to help you and other people in the room stay calm? The typical devotional time at the start of a church meeting serves a dual purpose. It calls up an awareness of God's presence—a very calming thought—and it may help participants start with a lower level of stress in case the meeting becomes tense. Clergy with this awareness might stop in the middle of meeting to offer prayer or use a mindfulness exercise like the ones in this book. In the middle of a hard conversation with a staff person, a trauma-informed pastor would intentionally lower tensions in the room by getting up and walking around for a little while or taking a bathroom break.

Check Your Pulse

At a time when you feel anxious, agitated, or shaky, check your pulse by hand, smartphone, or fitness device. Sit comfortably and quietly for a few minutes and let your eyes close or soften your gaze. Let thoughts that come up scroll past the visual screen in your mind without grabbing on to them or following them. Picture a relaxing word or scene in your visual field. Consciously take deep, long breaths that activate your chest and belly for several minutes. Use any of the breathing techniques you've read about and used earlier in the book. After ten minutes, take your pulse rate again. Experiment with how long you need to rest and breathe deeply to lower your heart rate; everyone is different. Do the exercise frequently for best results.

I find no truer verse from the Hebrew Scriptures than the psalmist's reverent reflection on the body: "I am fearfully and wonderfully made" (Ps 139:14). Our bodies have multiple complex response systems that work to keep us safe. Many functions alert us to present and future dangers. Understanding the physiology of trauma helps us reduce the impact of primary and secondary trauma in our lives and in the lives of people we serve. When these systems become exhausted from overuse, we need to get professional care for our physical and mental health. But before we get to exhaustion and burnout, we can build up trauma immunity by knowing our unique distress signals. As we increase daily self-care, we are more protected when intense situations inevitably come along.

CHAPTER NINE

TRANSGENERATIONAL TRAUMA
LEGACIES OF SILENCE AND CALLS FOR REPAIR

This pain feels very old, Sophia. Guide me as I seek to heal the fear responses in my body that have come from generations before me, including the fears created by America's legacy of racial violence and oppression. Equip me to give voice to family silences, to honor past injuries, and to liberate future generations from shame. Help me to see you everywhere—in brown skin, gender ambivalence, curvy hips, wide girth, black braids, tattoos, rosy cheeks, wide noses, narrow eyes—in unfamiliar faces, and in the mirror where I look each morning. May I be the body and soul where reparation is made.

In 1942, after the bombing of Pearl Harbor, the United States entered World War II. Fears immediately grew about Japanese Americans threatening national security. The War Relocation Authority (WRA) was established to oversee the wholesale roundup and incarceration of people of Japanese descent. They hired subcontractors to build ten camps to house 120,000 Japanese Americans.

I live within a two-hour drive of the camp at Tule Lake, California, which was the most prison-like (housing attempted escapees, deportees, and those who would not sign loyalty oaths or refused military service) and stayed open beyond the end of the war. Today, a run-down group of small, disintegrating wooden buildings can be seen from the road. A guard tower leans precariously, surrounded by barbed wire and chain link fencing. There is no museum at this site—there is nothing to proudly showcase from this dark chapter in US history—but it saddens me that no one has found a way to honor those who suffered and died at this camp. As the barracks fall further into disrepair, they tell the story of a brokenness and shame that incarceration inflicted on more than one generation.

As we study trauma's transgenerational impacts, we find two groups of people seeking trauma resolution and healing. We meet people whose parents, grandparents, and great-grandparents were enslaved, oppressed, abused, possessed, raped, incarcerated, and killed. They are calling for accurate historical narratives, validation for their loved ones' traumas, and the eradication of ongoing systemic injustices. We also find children, grandchildren and great-grandchildren whose forebearers were the oppressors who abused, possessed, raped, incarcerated, and killed people in America. They are trying to repair the sins of their forebearers. Both groups of generational trauma survivors carry visible and invisible scars from these traumas and from the silences and shame that followed them. The ongoing trauma in their bodies and souls is referred to as historical trauma and also called transgenerational trauma.

Trauma-informed clergy have a crucial role to play in telling true stories of these abuses and supporting efforts to heal the past, even when that involves atonement for Christian-sanctioned and -perpetrated genocide in our nation's history. While we cannot change the past, we can learn from it and thereby change the future. By understanding the shadows cast by the past upon victims and their families, trauma-informed pastoral care providers help survivors of transgenerational trauma (both perpetrators and victims) find peace and healing.

Transgenerational Trauma

Transgenerational trauma occurs when a traumatic experience (or group of experiences) greatly impacts more than one generation and lingers in their memories, bodies, and souls. Put more simply, trauma can be inherited. Subsequent generations react to perceived or actual fears and threats by listening to and observing their parents and grandparents. Neuroscience and epigenetics reveal physiological changes in the descendants of traumatized forebearers that can make them more vulnerable to traumatic stress.

OVERCOMING SILENCE AND SHAME

When my friend Morty was ten years old, his father designed and built one of the ten World War II incarceration camps. After the war, his family never spoke about it. In order to learn more about his family legacy, Morty went to a survivors' reunion at the camp his father built. "I went as an emissary for an apology from my father," he said. Descendants of slave owners, Civil War generals, Native American boarding school staff, Christian missionaries, Nazi guards, and sympathizers, among others, end up carrying the task of atonement and reparation. Many Americans have sought to repair family legacies by digging up the bones of their past. This is quite literally true in Tulsa, Oklahoma, where second-generation victims (descendants) of the Greenwood race massacre have come together to bring closure and healing by unearthing unmarked graves.

Two of Thomas Jefferson's great-grandsons have committed themselves to healing the past by asking officials to remove Jefferson's statues from public display. Lucian K. Truscott IV said, "I am the sixth-generation great-grandson of a slave owner. My cousins from the Sally Hemings family [an African slave who Jefferson owned and raped] are also the great-grandchildren of a slave owner." Truscott continues, "The time to honor the slave-owning founders of our imperfect union is past."[1] A sixth-generation great-grandson of Jefferson and Sally Hemings, Shannon LaNier, agrees: "Many statues of him should come down. He was, after all, a participant in the institution of slavery—perhaps the most notorious one among the Founding Fathers, not least because of the jarring contrast between what he practiced and what he preached."[2] Both men have chosen to look into their family story and change its false narratives. While they have done this on a public platform, many similar steps are being taken by ordinary people looking to overcome and heal their family's past.

As more than one verse in the Hebrew Scriptures says, the iniquity of the parents is visited "upon the children and the children's children, to the third and the fourth generation" (Exod 34:7).[3] There are multiple references to heritable suffering in Jewish and Christian writings. Shakespeare wrote his own well-known version, "The sins of the father are to be laid upon the children," in a race-biased discourse about Jews from *The Merchant of Venice*.[4] Shakespeare sadly misinterprets these texts as a curse against Jews, as have too many biblical scholars and preachers. I understand them to mean that sin and suffering are heritable and that each generation must atone for it and has an obligation to stop it.

In my work as a trauma-informed therapist, I have observed the truth within these verses. The burden of family shame falls on subsequent generations. To heal ourselves, we explore the past and repair what can yet be repaired. A parent's trauma can influence our mental health, career decisions, and partner choices. A grandparent's trauma can start a pattern of familial alcoholism, child abuse, and debilitating low self-esteem. Parental life choices influence our own lives for good or ill. What we do with their life stories is up to us, but if their choices have led to pain and suffering or affect future generations, it falls to us to heal those wounds.

TRANSGENERATIONAL TRAUMA AFFECTS

Morty went to the Japanese American survivors' reunion as a "witness" to the trauma his father's generation denied. The survivors' families had much more to grapple with and repair. Third-generation Japanese American (Sansei) Shirley Ann Higuchi, whose mother, Setsuko, was imprisoned at the Heart Mountain camp in Montana, has extensively collected stories about people in the camps. Her book *Setsuko's Secret* is the result of her research and describes her personal healing journey.[5] An attorney in Washington, DC, she hadn't expected to immerse herself in the past until her mother's death took her on a healing journey. As she studied victims' stories, what surprised her was the toll the incarceration experience had on survivors' children and grandchildren, many of whom are now examining their trauma legacy by immersing themselves in history.[6]

There are still many untold stories about the camps. Newspaper clippings from those years made it all look so much better than it was. Photographs show smiling Japanese Americans living in clean, small rooms. Guard towers, armed patrols, and barbed wire fences were notably cropped out. Only by learning names and hearing the stories of survivors and their descendants does their ordeal become clearer.

My friend's father, like other White Americans who were involved in or supported the incarceration, believed that his actions were justified, even patriotic, because he was doing his part for the war effort. People who worked at the camps, from construction teams to guards, had to deny the life-altering trauma they observed. The internment was "the culmination of the federal government's long history of racist and discriminatory treatment of Asian immigrants and their descendants that had begun with restrictive immigration policies in the late 1800s."[7]

Internees arrived at the camps in shock and grief. Within weeks after the Japanese bombing at Pearl Harbor, the FBI raided their homes; took their possessions, properties, and farmlands; and forcibly removed them from their communities. They were bused to temporary holding centers and then to various camps. Their homes and businesses were boarded up, and their assets sold for nearly nothing or frozen by the banks. Some of them hid possessions with friends who could keep them safe, but most lost cherished objects, prime farmland, and substantial wealth.

The trauma that incarceration placed on people of Japanese ancestry (two-thirds of them American citizens) left several generations with negative feelings about themselves and negative health outcomes. As many as 1,862 people died from multiple causes during their incarceration.[8] Living survivors from these camps have pushed the nation to reckon with this disgraceful past. In 1988, the US government said that internees had suffered a "grave injustice" and offered them an apology and monetary awards, twenty thousand dollars for each incarcerated person.[9] It must be noted that during wars with other nations (Germany and Italy), their American counterparts were not interned on a massive scale.

Long-term trauma symptoms stemming from these four to five years didn't end after the war. Racial bias against Japanese Americans made it difficult for them to reestablish their lives. Incarcerated first-generation Japanese (Issei) men who had immigrated to the United States faced ongoing health problems after the war ended. They were twice as likely to die before the age of sixty as men who were spared incarceration. Second-generation Japanese (Nisei) who were incarcerated as teenagers had low self-esteem, humiliation, and self-blame and long after the war exhibited symptoms similar to those reported by other racial trauma victims.[10]

Three generations of descendants (thus far studied) from incarcerated adults have felt the need to be superior Americans to make up for the humiliation of internment, adopting English and setting aside Japanese language and ethnic identity. Many focused on becoming high achievers and model citizens. The pressure to become "super (Asian) Americans" grew, in part, from attempts to overcome incarceration and shame after the war.[11]

After traumatic experiences, perpetrators and victims alike avoid talking about their trauma. Japanese survivors' silences meant that most of their children were raised with secrets about the camp.[12] So was my friend Morty, whose father built one of those camps. Parents intentionally hide many personally painful stories. Perpetrators of racial violence keep silent to avoid shame and guilt, leaving victims with their perpetrators' unhealed and often unrepentant shame.

Many trauma victims/survivors keep their stories to themselves, leaving subsequent generations clueless about the pain they inherit but can't clearly find a source for. War veterans keep silent for years, and some carry their stories to their graves. Survivors are often just trying to protect themselves from reawakened traumatic memories—but they also keep silent to protect their children, whom they don't want to burden with the sadness of the past.

Survivors fear that talking about their trauma will reawaken horrific memories. But silence doesn't effectively keep trauma at bay. At one hundred and seven years old, Viola Fletcher, who was seven when a White mob devastated her Greenwood, Oklahoma, community, recently decided to end her years of silence. One hundred years ago, she witnessed the sixteen-hour terror of White men shooting Black men, women, and children on the streets and her neighborhood set ablaze. Ten thousand people were displaced and destitute thereafter. She testified before Congress on the centennial anniversary of the massacre, along with other survivors and descendants who are asking for economic restitution. Her soul wounds cannot be so easily repaired. She said, "I still see Black men being shot, Black bodies lying in the street. I still smell smoke and see fire. . . . I still hear airplanes flying overhead. . . . I hear the screams. I have lived through the massacre every day. Our country may forget this history, but I cannot."[13]

Studies have shown that transgenerational trauma survivors' mental health varies depending on how much they think about the pain and injustice done to their people in the past.[14] With too little information, victims and their adult children are left to ruminate and obsess about what might have happened and must search for lost personal and cultural identity. When too much time and thought is given to rumination about past trauma, descendants respond with increased physiological stress and feelings of shame and hopelessness. For some people, the more they think about these historic losses, the more disempowered they become. For others, fully disclosed history provides wisdom and healing. A balance appears to be needed between no talk at all and too much talk that is focused on highly traumatic elements within family stories. For second- and third-generation offspring, their parents' silences seem to have protected them and coincidentally left them a confusing and disconcerting trauma legacy they now need to heal.

PAIN: YOURS, MINE, OURS

Our shared humanity includes traumatic suffering, recovery, and resilience. In the popular public television series program *Finding Your Roots*, historian Henry Louis Gates Jr. guides his guests back through time. Learning previously untold stories adds a richness and depth to their identities that leaves participants and viewers in tears. Coming to grips with the real past enables us all to look at today quite differently. In her book *Caste*, Isabelle Wilkerson uses a metaphor comparing the developed world to an old falling-down house: "None of us was here when this house was built. Our immediate ancestors may have had nothing to do with it, but here we are, the current occupants of a property with stress cracks and bowed walls and fissures built into the foundation. We are the heirs to whatever is right or wrong with it. . . . Any further deterioration is, in fact, on our hands."[15] In trauma care, we recognize and validate the need for restoration and repair.

As we each become familiar with the trauma legacy within our families, we have a very real touchstone from which to care for others. Let's take a minute to think about groups of people who have experienced past and ongoing trauma in America: African slaves, indentured Irish immigrants, Jewish descendants of the Holocaust, Indigenous and First Nations people, Latinx immigrants, and Asian Americans. Many other communities carry transgenerational trauma: Hmong, Vietnamese, Iraqi and Afghan immigrants who served alongside US soldiers during wartime. There are too many groups to name. When I think about the ancestry pie chart people get from an analysis of their DNA, I imagine many segments with trauma histories.

Most US immigrant stories begin with violent ethnic cleansing, abject poverty, political upheaval, or war. People come here from all over the world to escape repeated traumas, and it means leaving behind anything too big to be carried on their backs or in a suitcase or duffel bag. They borrow money from friends and family to pay for the journey or go into debt or voluntary servitude. Most leave family members behind—possibly forever—and say good-bye to loved ones. Indentured Europeans, as well as freedom-seeking adventurers, bring trauma legacies of interethnic cleansing and religious persecution to the shores of North America.[16] Upon arrival, traumatized immigrants are retraumatized by racist harassment, mandated English language use, and barriers to housing and employment. Assimilation becomes more or less challenging for them depending on their placement in the caste system here in the United States.

Some transgenerational trauma survivors relegated to the lowest caste live with an understandably bitter belief (and observed experience) that the American dream will never be available to or achieved by them. This is true for both the descendants of immigrants and the descendants of slaves. Joyce DeGruy describes the disillusionment for adult descendents of slaves (ADOS): "From the beginning,

Africans were taught they were inferior, physically, emotionally, intellectually, and spiritually, thus rendering them completely ineffectual in their own eyes and in the eyes of the society around them. . . . Since the abolition of slavery, such notions have continued to infiltrate all aspects of American life."[17] Racial trauma leads to negative mental health outcomes in most cultural groups in America. Persistent negation, microaggressions, and racial bias in public discourse all add to a collective belief that this abuse will continue through even more generations.

Releasing

As you read about trauma's long-lasting impacts, you may notice changes in the rhythm of your breathing. Bring your attention to the flow of your in breath and out breath. Take easy, natural in breaths and release them slowly, like the movement of the sea. Let your body relax into the rocking and caressing of these breaths. Let thoughts fade into the distance like boats on the horizon as you sit quietly and pause in your reading. As you do this breathwork, let the peace you experience spread out in a gentle way to touch your ancestors' pain and release it into Divine care. Slowly return to awareness of the place where you now sit and gently breathe. Close your eyes for a few minutes and then continue reading.

NATIVE AMERICAN AND INDIGENOUS CULTURAL TRAUMA

One of the oldest historical traumas in our nation began with the Indian Removal Act of 1830. It promised to give eastern tribal nations new lands in the West, resulting in the relocation of one hundred thousand Native Americans. Between 1900 and 1957, more than eighty Indigenous tribes were completely wiped out through disease and genocide.[18] As early European White settlers (under the banner of Christian dominion) encroached on sovereign lands and destroyed Native and Indigenous cultures, their self-justifying genocide simultaneously supported the institution of slavery. Martin Luther King Jr., all too familiar with generational trauma among Black people, wrote, "Our nation was born in genocide. . . . We are perhaps the only nation which tried as a matter of national policy to wipe out its indigenous population. Moreover, we elevated that tragic experience into a noble crusade. Indeed, even today we have not permitted ourselves to reject or feel remorse for this shameful episode. Our literature, our films, our drama, our folklore all exalt it."[19]

Under a banner of righteousness and moral supremacy, Christian clergy, congregations, and denominations participated in tribal genocide. More than a dozen different Christian denominations ran boarding schools from 1860 to 1978, established with the aim of solving what they called, the "Indian problem," by civilizing them. The long-term psychological impact of this abuse is felt yet today.

In an essay about her Ojibwe mother's forced attendance at a Catholic Indian school on the Odanah reservation in northern Wisconsin, Mary Annette Pember writes, "Like most Native American peoples, our family's story is touched by the legacy of boarding schools, institutions created to destroy and vilify Native culture, language, family, and spirituality." Mary believes that her mother's reluctance to talk about the school stems from her indescribably painful trauma. Like other adults I have described in this chapter, Mary has spent her adulthood trying to uncover her mother's hidden past in order to understand her transgenerational trauma legacy. She says, "I am consumed by the need to validate and prove, intellectually and emotionally, [my mother's] experiences . . . in the face of generations of federal and Church denials in their role in the boarding schools' brutality."

Mary describes what "civilizing" her mother meant in practice: "Students were stripped of all things associated with Native life." Their traditional long hair was cut, their clothing was replaced by school uniforms, and students were "physically punished for speaking their Native languages." Their attachment bonds were totally severed: "Contact with family and community members was discouraged or forbidden altogether. Survivors have described a culture of pervasive physical and sexual abuse at the schools. Food and medical attention were often scarce; many students died. Their parents sometimes learned of their death only after they had been buried in school cemeteries, some of which were unmarked."[20]

The destruction of cultural norms, values, faith traditions, and native languages so greatly damaged a whole generation's self-esteem that tribal communities have faced insurmountable odds in trying to recover. Descendants are still reeling from the length and breadth of this trauma. Transgenerational trauma symptoms in tribal communities underlie substance abuse, domestic violence, and poor health outcomes among Native and Indigenous people. Some populations in the Native American community are suffering from "severe emotional, physical and social-environmental consequences related to past traumas."[21] While all Native American people and their experiences are not the same, persistent symptoms of chronic stress are observed by therapists and researchers. In an article for *Counselor* magazine, Kathleen Brown-Rice writes, "The traumatic events suffered during previous generations creates a pathway that results in the current generation being at an increased risk of experiencing mental and physical distress that leaves them unable to gain strength from their indigenous culture or utilize their natural familial and tribal support system."[22]

Church-Sponsored Boarding Schools

Take time to search the internet for a list of denominations and religious organizations that sponsored Indian boarding schools. Was yours on the list? Was there a boarding school within your judicatory area or near your faith community? What has your denomination done to explore, acknowledge, and repair abuses that took place at these boarding schools? If you aren't sure, make it a priority to learn more. What might you do to educate your faith community about this transgenerational trauma? Reach out to tribal elders in your area who can teach you and your congregation more about abuses at these schools. Ask them about ways to repent and repair.[23]

HOW WE LEARN ABOUT FAMILY TRAUMA

Some people who carry transgenerational trauma delve into the past to dig up truths about their families, especially when family stories are obscured by silences and secrets. But even without the "facts," children learn by observation. They learn by rules that define subjects that can be discussed and subjects that can't. They learn through their parents' emotional reactions and strong feelings. Children are influenced by their parents' thoughts, feelings, and behaviors when something tragic takes place and when life falls apart afterward.

Without knowing much about the past, adults stumble into behaviors that resemble parental patterns. An overly protected daughter may not know that her mother was sexually traumatized, but she will sense her mother's extreme anxiety when she begins to date. A man who is a third-generation descendent of family poverty begins to understand the impact of this legacy when he is told that he'll never amount to anything and that he shouldn't aim his sights too high. Many adults have learned about their parents' trauma by unconsciously replicating their thoughts, feelings, and behaviors.

Along with inherited psychological patterns, it is also quite possible that people whose parents lived through intensely traumatic experiences have inherited physiological stress vulnerability. I've previously described trauma's physiology. To recap, when we are in danger—either literal or imaginative—our bodies quickly respond. Our lungs expand with oxygen, and our adrenal glands release epinephrine and cortisol, which speed up our hearts and raise our blood pressure to help us fight, run, or play dead. All of these systems work together to enable a quick response. This response system is called the hypothalamic-pituitary-adrenal (HPA) axis. Prolonged trauma throws this system into chaos; it changes the body's adrenal activation and shuts down ordinary response systems, especially when it occurs during early development.[24]

Extensive research has been conducted on the transgenerational transmission of trauma borne by Holocaust victims and their descendants. The children of Holocaust survivors appear to have markedly lower cortisol levels than children in the general population. Changes have been observed in the size and function of the amygdala after repeated traumatic experiences. These studies provide significant evidence that trauma exposure in one generation changes the function of the HPA in the next, putting subsequent generations at increased risk for PTSD symptoms.[25] Another group of studies found that changes to the activation of DNA in one generation can affect the on and off switches within the HPA in the next, leaving offspring with increased vulnerabilities. Scientists in the field of epigenetics are exploring (and debating) this possibility, which has tremendous implications for transgenerational trauma survivors. Trauma experiences in one lifetime could be followed by more than one change to fight/flight/freeze responses in the next.[26] If more research proves that this is true, the Bible's ancient wisdom is correct: the sin-inflicted trauma in one generation is physiologically laid upon the next to the third and fourth generations.

STARTING PLACES FOR HEALING

Trauma-informed clergy make time to explore the trauma in their own families. My forebearers came to the United States with enough money to buy them safe passage and a plot of land. They were German and Scotch-Irish, and I have little history about their decision to come here or their assimilation challenges. But I have explored the trauma my grandfather experienced because it showed up unbidden when I was making a tough midlife career decision. At forty-one, I discerned a new call to leave parish ministry and become a therapist, but in order to enroll in a doctoral program, I would burden my future with what seemed like insurmountable debt. I was a single mother on an associate pastor's salary, paying for my daughter's college education. To go back to school myself, I'd have to let go of a consistent paycheck and face financial insecurity. I became extremely anxious, lost sleep, and almost gave up the dream. I could either let my fear turn me away from my goal or turn toward my fear and examine it. I found its origins in the past.

My parents had always been extremely frugal, avoiding credit cards and never letting a bill become overdue. My father traded career advancement for career security. I learned from him and developed a large fear that I could be destitute at any moment. Where did this family "bag lady" come from? I had to go farther up the family tree to put the pieces together.

My grandfather on my father's side was orphaned at age twelve when his father was run over by a train while collecting coal to heat the family home, and his mother was thereafter murdered by a man she refused to marry. Grandfather was left to care for his four younger siblings, who survived by selling newspapers and working odd jobs. They slept beneath bridges and stole food. The oldest girl found a boy who could give her a better life and ran off with him. The younger boys stuck with my grandfather who raised them and eventually paid for their college educations. By the age of thirty, he had obtained an advanced degree and opened a successful business, but he was forever emotionally scarred by the fear destitution had understandably planted in his soul. Grandfather's fear became my father's fear and then became my fear. Only by finding its transgenerational roots could I consciously choose to conquer it.

By examining our family histories back through as many generations as we can and seeing the suffering our ancestors endured, we can find insights about our character, feelings, anxieties, and behaviors. We need to explore the past because what we don't know (and are not told) about our family trauma can hurt us. Healing transgenerational wounds can be a gift to generations that follow us.

Faith communities can help individuals with this exploration by gathering them together to write essays about their families or bring photos to talk about. Aging members in congregations may already be engaged in life review and documenting family stories for future generations. We can encourage congregants to talk about traumatic elements in their family stories and then broaden the discussion to include historic and present trauma in their communities. Clergy and lay leaders can invite diverse activists, writers, and poets to come and speak about their transgenerational trauma. These conversations will deepen relationships among participants and foster empathy.

Along the way, we will discover additional pathways to healing. We can be allies with people who are working to end patterns of racial oppression and violence in our country. Refugee sponsorship has long been the work of faith-based organizations, congregations, and individuals who understand trauma and work to alleviate it. We can support and expand these acts of love and service.

We can lift up and celebrate the resilience in each individual and culture. Psalm 34:18 proclaims, "The Lord is near to the brokenhearted, and saves the crushed in spirit." A Latgawa woman once told me that in order to heal her transgenerational trauma, her tribal elder instructed her to dance, drum, and sing every single day. This is one path by which to be healed and become a healer.

CONNECTING THE PAST TO THE PRESENT

By stopping today's trauma, we honor yesterday's victims. For their sake, we are compelled to ask, "What is happening in America today that will leave future generations less traumatized than they are now?" And we ask, "How, when, and where is abuse still being justified by my local or denominational faith community?" We can challenge our congregants to recognize and change trauma-inducing disparities today, including injustices in health care and family separations along our borders.[27] And it is up to us to connect dehumanizing policies, racial stereotyping, and inequitable resource distribution to their roots in our nation's past.

Transgenerational trauma studies connect the dots for us. Anti-Asian immigration discrimination in the 1800s is connected to internment camps in World War II and hate crimes against Asians communities today. Slavery's trauma is connected to decades-long discrimination against American descendants of slavery (ADOS), including current barriers to housing, education, and health care, along with aggressive treatment by the police and inequity in the criminal justice system. Broken US treaties, genocide, and church-sponsored culture suppression is connected to poverty, domestic violence, and alcoholism among Native and Indigenous people today. Generational poverty and economic insecurity among lower-caste European White people are connected to fears that Latinx and Mexican immigrants will replace them in the workforce, and those fears lead to traumatizing policies and procedures at the Mexican border. We are called to keep connecting the dots in order to break these cycles of violence and trauma.

We have to resist disempowerment that says, "We'll never be able to change these patterns!" Can we apologize for something we didn't do? Yes. Clergy and congregations are in a uniquely powerful position from which to do this. By saying that what our forebearers in faith did was against everything we believe in, we begin to right terrible wrongs. By saying, "I'm sorry that happened to you (or your family)," very specifically and owning the trauma perpetuated by our faith communities, we create cultural change. For example, some of the clergy in my county begin worship by honoring ancestors, saying, "We are gathered today on the ancestral homelands of the Shasta, Takelma, and Latgawa tribes." Virginia Theological Seminary is leading by example. They have promised to pay financial reparation to the descendants of slaves who built their facilities, expand their Black studies programs, and support historically Black congregations in their area.

Following Martin Luther King Jr.'s prophetic call to feel remorse for past afflictions, congregations can work in collaboration with healing groups formed by survivors and their descendants.[28] We can learn more about reconciling and healing actions. It is our job to ask victims, "What (if anything) can we do to repair the damage?"

It is then our job to treat what we hear as sacred, to reflect on it, and to take action. We can develop and adopt official statements of apology and encourage denominational leaders to do the same.

These healing steps might be met with resistance. While writing this chapter, I had a phone call with an old friend, and I mentioned the painful things I was writing about. He was adamant that there was nothing that he could do about America's brutal past. "I wasn't there, and I can't go back there," he said. The conversation left me disquieted. When people ignore the trauma experienced by others, they remain isolated by cultural privilege. As we become trauma-informed, clergy and faith communities are called on to acknowledge, repair, and heal transgenerational trauma. As we take in the transgenerational pain around us, "Who is my neighbor?" becomes "What can I do to alleviate my neighbor's pain?"

CHAPTER TEN
SPIRITUAL CARE THROUGH THE TRAUMA LENS

Way beyond all journeying, truth behind all mystery, life within all living:
WE PRAISE YOU.
Salve for every soreness, mender of every brokenness, midwife of a better future:
WE PRAISE YOU.
Ground of all being, judge of all nations, conscience of the universe:
WE PRAISE YOU.
Maker, Redeemer, confessor, companion, befriender, inspirer, God beyond all names:
WE PRAISE YOU.
                    —"Morning Liturgy B," The Iona Community

I volunteered as a small-town hospice chaplain during my first years in full-time pastoral ministry, perhaps a bit overly confident that my clinical pastoral education was sufficient preparation for this work. Visiting a very sick woman at the hospital one day, I prayed at her bedside, and then I took a breather. Her daughter saw me in the hallway and took me aside to tell me that her mother was a lifelong alcoholic in the end stages of liver failure. The next day, I sat opposite the husband at the dying woman's bed. As she slept soundly, I told him that I was sorry that his life had included the challenges her drinking had presented. I immediately knew by his body language that this was the wrong thing to say. He bluntly asked me to never mention it to him or to anyone else and then he asked me to leave the room. It was a tough way to learn the power of denial!

DENIAL AND TRAUMA

It wasn't until I was in a graduate school psychology classroom that I changed my largely negative attitude about denial. In the late 1800s, Sigmund Freud proposed the theory that people use defense mechanisms to keep from feeling anxiety about unwanted or unacceptable feelings. He called one of them denial, a concept that his daughter, Anna, elaborated in 1936. Denial defends us when the truth is too painful to accept. For example, a woman who is told that her son has died in battle desperately believes that he is missing in action instead. Even when presented with overwhelming evidence, she rejects it to keep from collapsing under the weight of the truth. Her denial protects her. It keeps her from feeling terrifying emotions and helps her to slowly take in traumatic information, one piece at a time.

In a similar way, the husband whose wife was dying of liver failure from her excessive drinking had lived in denial about her alcoholism for many years, and he was not going to let go of it as she lay dying. The thought of abandoning her or being without her had been too painful to face. He felt angry, guilty, and resentful about their lost years, so he used denial as a protective partner against the truth. Only after she died could he possibly crack open the deep wounds he felt throughout the last years of their lives together. As he grieved, I hope his daughter, a prayer partner, or a support group helped him learn more about his pain. I learned to check my assumptions about anyone else's life journey before I offer a viewpoint disguised as compassion.

We all use denial. On a typical day, denial keeps us going. In the morning, we get dressed, shower, drink a cup of coffee, eat a little something, read a devotional or the morning news, and head on out. If we didn't have denial, we couldn't do it. We would think about the odds of getting in a traffic accident as we start up the car, then turn it off and go back inside. We would avoid the grocery store until the very last drop of milk was gone in case a random shooter sprayed the store with bullets. We would never say good-bye to our partner, child, parent, or pet without fearing that this would be our last hug. Denial helps us get out the door and stays with us through the day. Trauma destroys protective denial. For the child living in a tent under a bridge, the woman who is drugged and raped, the transgender person beaten on a subway platform, the widow who lost her young husband in the pandemic, the evacuated person who returns to find his house in ruins, it's hard to feel safe. They think "It can happen," "It can happen to me!" and "It can happen to someone I love." They know that life is short, violence prevails, and every day is challenging and uncertain. They feel extremely vulnerable. Going out the door each day (which most of us do casually) becomes difficult because since "it" happened, "it" could happen again. And "it" means *anything* violent, deadly, tragic, or life-changing. The fear of recurrent trauma has nothing to do with calculated risk or facts and evidence. Those make not one whit of difference. Trauma has stripped away all pretenses.

UPENDED FAITH

Trauma similarly impacts faith. Under normal circumstances, belief in God, a higher power, an ever-present holy spirit, or inner guide can be protective. People who attend religious services and are supported by faith communities have better overall mental health than those who don't. Helpful expressions of spirituality that "encourage personal empowerment . . . and promote the importance of emotions such as hope, forgiveness and purpose" can enhance healing and promote mental health.[1] Some trauma victims utilize their previous belief systems and faith communities during recovery. Others find that trauma has totally upended their faith, and they toss out all previously held theological constructs and beliefs. When the bomb exploded and they saw the aftermath, when their child was molested, when their father drowned in his car trying to escape rising floodwaters, when Covid-19 took the life of a young friend, when gun violence killed another neighbor, maintaining faith in God's promises often became totally impossible.

Trauma leads people smack-dab into hard questions about life: "Why is life so damned random?" "Why did I survive when others didn't?" "Why is God punishing me?" Psychologist Robert Grant, in his book *The Way of the Wound*, notes, "All victims, in a way that is initially unclear, are asked to confront life's most difficult challenges and, in the process, to discover both the Spirit and their deeper Self."[2] People with repeated trauma experiences are especially inclined to give up on a previously rich relationship with God. What former beliefs do victims reconsider? God either cannot protect us or chooses not to. Both explanations are unsatisfactory. After a tragedy, some survivors believe that God has not kept his promises. Others conclude that they didn't deserve to be spared. They can feel utterly abandoned, and they may push back or push away from God for the rest of their lives.

In my earlier book on trauma, I proposed that trauma survivors ask questions in three main categories: "Why me?" "Why evil?" and "Why God?"[3] They turn to clergy to explore questions they typically wouldn't raise with anyone else—not with their family members and not with therapists, who may not share their religious perspectives. If they have a trusting relationship with their rabbi or pastor, they will ask, "Where was God when this happened?" "How do I find meaning and purpose for my life again?" "What is God calling me to do now?" Trauma-trained clergy recognize that such questions are spiritual "quests" arising out of and linked to very deep wounds, and they resist the temptation to answer them.

When patients in my psychotherapy office wanted me to answer their hard spiritual questions after traumatic loss, I would gently say, "I could answer that question for you, but it would come from my journey rather than yours. It might be the best answer for me, but not the best answer for you." And then I would offer to stay alongside them as they puzzled over, raged against, sat in the dark with, or otherwise reexamined their faith and life journey.

Providing pastoral care for victims who are open to spiritual exploration—and more vulnerable than they may have ever been—requires patience and far more listening than talking. Victims know intuitively how to reconstruct faith when things fall apart. They are teachers for anyone trying to help them. In a note written for judicatory clergy who interview sexual abuse survivors, clergy abuse survivor Randy Ellison wrote, "I would strongly suggest that in the hour prior to any [conversation with] a survivor you should meditate or pray focusing on humility. When a survivor speaks their truth, it is coming from the soul, which in my book is as close to God as you can get. Leave your egos, and your Jesus complexes behind."[4]

Trying to answer gut-wrenching existential questions can be uncomfortable for victims and pastoral care providers alike. After all, we are preachers and teachers, chaplains and counselors who have extensively studied Scripture; we're supposed to interpret God's messages and translate them into everyday language. Some of us speak for God every week! We will make a mess of it with trauma survivors, however, unless we readily admit our incognizance. Victims have been unwittingly thrown into an exploration process and need to find their own answers to big existential questions.

By letting victims know we don't have answers and *definitely* don't know which answers are right for them, we affirm their present condition and join them in the search for meaning. We may end up feeling as lost and helpless as they feel. Their journey may upend *our* faith, which is why many clergy avoid sitting in angst alongside trauma survivors. It would be psychologically simpler to offer platitudes, pass them a Scripture verse, or offer a prayer from a prayer book. Doing that would keep us safely distant if we are too frightened to delve into pain and doubt.

What if this interpersonal journey with someone in deep pain strips away *our* denial? What if it taps into *our* own known or unknown trauma? What if *our* faith gets shaky, and it all begins to fall apart? Is it worth the risk? I believe it is. Loving others in times of joy or in their deepest sorrows is the essence of our call. Although it takes us, as it took the ancient goddess Psyche, down through layers of darkness, we will come out with greater peace, compassion, and wisdom. It is worth the risk. When any of our old conventional theologies no longer serve to speak to the world's traumas, we need to go on our own healing exploration, or we need to stop preaching.

SHAME OR GRACE?

In multiple studies, religion is shown to benefit overall mental health, *except* when it is overly simplistic, dogmatic, and shame inducing.[5] Dismissive or hurtful comments by members of faith communities can devastate trauma victims. When their pain is disbelieved, they are blamed, or they are told to get over a wound that lingers, their recovery is delayed. A faith community can't offer healing benefits to victims unless the community conveys more grace than shame during trauma care.

Clergy and faith leaders need to honor victims' doubts, disbeliefs, and lack of concrete answers. Many of us have been taught that suffering is a sign of faithlessness rather than a period of rich spiritual engagement. When people around victims equate the victims' pain with a *lack* of anything, we do them a great disservice and impede recovery.

Think for a minute about the unhelpful comments made by Job's friends in the Hebrew Scriptures. After Job is repeatedly traumatized— by losing family members, his wealth, his status in the community, his spiritual grounding, and his health—his friends come along to offer him some advice. They start out by doing the right thing; they sit in silence with Job for seven days. And then they go way off track and begin talking. They tell him that his suffering is his own fault. This protects them from thinking, "Oh, my God, this could happen to me!" And they emotionally distance themselves from Job's pain by offering him pat answers, most of which blame or shame him. This ancient story illustrates what commonly happens in well-meaning but nevertheless abusive faith communities. Through direct comments or by way of gossip, victims are blamed for their suffering: Black and Brown people for resisting police officers who are abusive, LGBTQ people for being thrown out of their families of origin, Asian people for spreading a deadly virus, alcoholic or mentally ill people for their houselessness, women who are date-raped for drinking at a party, and so on. Victims who encounter blame and retraumatization in faith communities lose trust in religious organizations altogether, step away to protect themselves, and often never reconnect.

There is a better approach. When congregations come alongside trauma victims with grace and compassion even though the journey can be painful and messy, they draw a wider circle of care. When they take time to study and understand trauma, they are more likely to provide appropriate care. Clergy leaders can offer resources to their congregations by hosting small-group book studies, telling stories of trauma survivors in newsletters and in worship, and inviting victim advocacy groups to make presentations. Trauma-informed clergy build up trauma-informed faith communities.

When victims are encouraged to go on quests to find answers to hard questions rather than given platitudes, they are supported in their healing. In Job's case, he simply ignored his "congregation" and took his questions directly to God. But I have seen faith communities and clergy who are tuned in to the needs of trauma survivors. They provide safe spaces for victims to express doubts, to lament, to rail against injustice while staying in healthy relational connection throughout the healing process. For example, a congregation in New York City organized survivor groups around the theme of mending. With old worn sweaters on their laps, participants learned to crochet, knit, or hand stitch to make the garment whole again. As they patched sweaters, they patched lives. Faith communities can be powerful places of solace and healing. In small groups where faith questions are viewed as healthy and spiritually enlightening, victims feel safe, and mending begins.

WHEN CHILDLIKE FAITH FAILS

Worn down by stress and emotionally overwhelmed, some trauma victims avoid complex faith questions by grasping at old childhood beliefs. I recall being told at seminary that most Christians stop their faith growth at the age of thirteen. This is ironically the age at which television producers target contents and language for their sitcom audiences. On any given Sunday, you and I can find simplistic answers at a number of nearby churches. Those churches are drawing large crowds and urging them to follow the concrete and unequivocal answers they will find in their Bibles. They ask their followers to trust their preachers and ruling (typically male) leaders, who are happy to provide answers to their questions. The preaching message boils down to this: have greater faith. Doubt is the devil's work. This is another example of a shame-based theology that disrupts healing for trauma survivors, who see wagging fingers pointed in their direction. Some believers prefer simple answers and cling to their childhood faith.

Not me. Kneeling on the floor beside me with her elbows on my childhood bed, my mother taught me to fold my hands, bow my head, and offer this prayer: "Now I lay me down to sleep, I pray the Lord my soul to keep, if I should die before I wake, I pray the Lord my soul to take." It terrified me in childhood, and it has always sounded more like a threat than a comfort. It offered me no help at all when I was an adult in the emergency room at my local hospital. After reviewing an X-ray, the ER doctor closed the door to my room, sagged down in the chair next to me, and told me that I had a rapidly growing, untreatable cancer. On that day, the God of my childhood who was all powerful, masculine, and strong enough to hold the whole world in his hands was apparently somewhere else.

How would I find comfort as I took in such terrible news? I had to go inward and live with my anxiety, to find God sitting with me there. I discarded much of what a whole lifetime of preachers had been telling me from their safe, privileged pulpits. It wasn't until I lay down on a mountain path alongside a stream ("he leads me beside still waters," Ps 23:2) that I found peace. And the experience was so inwardly powerful that I can explain it more poetically than literally. Lying on the path in stillness, I felt the sun shooting through me into the soil. I felt my body disappearing and my soul becoming one with the air, shadows, yellow monkey flowers on the rock wall next to me. The peace I felt was overwhelmingly beautiful. I was reassured that when I died, I could feel like I did that day, blissfully at one with the earth, sky, and God.

Exploring Your Quests

When has a life moment sent you on a quest? What did you find along the way? Did you doubt the existence of God? What caused your dark nights of the soul? When have you felt all alone and abandoned by God? When have you felt flooded with peace and reassurance?

After three uncertain years that included an invasive surgery, multiple scans, and blood tests, my condition turned out to be a trauma-inducing *false* medical diagnosis. I am filled with relief and gratitude, not only that I am well, but for the moment I experienced on that mountain path. Medical trauma threw me into a spiritual crisis that allowed me to free myself from simplistic answers and final remnants of my childhood religion. I ditched my mother's bedtime prayer, along with her belief in predestination. I also discarded some of my adult learning. I tossed out three years of seminary education wherein White European theologians—who lived at the top of the caste system—posited complex ideas about suffering and redemption. I abandoned classical atonement theories. My suffering did not seem to be inflicted for my salvation, and all I wanted from Jesus was for him to show me the way to the abundant joy he promised. My old-time religion was all heady left-brain stuff, and I was in a right-brain trauma frame of mind. When it came right down to it, no theology I had previously subscribed to sufficed.

What I gained by facing death was a visceral sense that God is present and will always be present with me, even—and particularly—when I am in great pain or inner turmoil. Recapturing my experience as I write it down today, I feel calm. I can pull up this moment in my mind at any time I am anxious or afraid.

Releasing "Haa"

Close your eyes or soften your gaze. Take three or four comfortable breaths. On your next breath, take a large breath in, then breathe out with your jaw relaxed, and say a quick and powerful "haa" to release the rest of your air. Let stillness and peace arise in a "hold" at the end of the out breath. Do this a few times before moving on.

SCRIPTURE AND HEALING

You have the blessed opportunity to companion people as they heal. As you listen to victims' doubts and despair and learn about their quests and their questions, you can help them in more concrete ways. To promote trauma healing, start with the wealth of resources you have at your fingertips. If they don't want to explore Scripture, offer them a book, a poem, a meditation app, or even a film or podcast that provides insights on suffering and recovery.

As with other aspects in trauma-informed care, avoid making assumptions about any person's faith or faith background. Open inquiry will give you more information about the survivor's perspectives and current needs. For people who find Scripture helpful, start by offering them themes rather than selected verses. Avoid content that equates suffering to faithlessness or is otherwise shame inducing. When someone cries out for justice, point them to biblical characters who take issue with God. To honor a victim's anger at God for abandoning them, direct them to verses where the writers also demand answers.

Many people raised in Jewish and Christian faith communities are used to finding their own stories in Scripture. Hebrew and Christian texts are rich with images of trauma and restoration. When victims come to you with doubts, encourage them to read about people who survived against all odds. A woman named Rachel embraced her lamentation; slaves in Egypt found their way to a land of milk and honey. Ruth, lost in grief after her husband's death, turned to her mother-in-law and received unconventional help.

The Psalms provide an abundance of insights. Tucked into Psalm 139, after beautiful testimony about God's care and providence, is a rarely read verse that validates the rage and anger many victims feel and express after being wounded by a gunman, a drunk driver, or a rapist: "I hate them with perfect hatred; I count them my enemies" (v. 22). This verse assures survivors who have been deeply wounded that their strong feelings are normal. Decrying evil is part of the faith journey. The Psalms help trauma victims by balancing strong negative emotions with gratitude and hope. The psalmist often holds two opposite emotions at the same time. Protest and praise both appear in a single psalm, unapologetically.

When theologian and poet Ann Weems's son Todd was killed less than an hour past his twenty-first birthday, she was devastated. In her journey to recover from this loss, she rewrote the Psalms from a survivor's viewpoint. I have often recommended her book to people coping with traumatic loss. She describes both deep pain and incremental recovery. In the preface of her book *Psalms of Lament*, she writes:

In the godforsaken, obscene quicksand of life,
there is a deafening alleluia
rising from the souls
of those who weep,
and those who weep with those who weep.
If you watch, you will see
the hand of God
putting the stars back in their skies
one by one.[6]

PRAYER IN TRAUMA CARE

When pastors and chaplains pray during trauma, spiritual, psychological, and physical changes take place in quite literally every body. Let's go back to the scene of chaplain Rear Admiral Margaret Grun Kibben who was offering prayers at the US Capitol during the invasion when she offered her frightened "congregation" a reminder that God is present. Kibben said, "God's got this,"[7] and in so doing, she counteracted racing thoughts such as "We aren't safe," "It's out of control," and "I could die here today." For those who were listening, she cut through the rush of adrenaline and cortisol they were experiencing and helped them focus on escape procedures. People in the room could calm down a bit by thinking "someone (God, Spirit, Divine Presence) more powerful than I am will deliver me to safety." Even a slight shift in their arousal systems changed their thoughts from panic's powerlessness to a calmer trust that they could and would survive, allowing their reactions to shift from instinctual to intentional.

During intense trauma, people gather themselves in prayer. Crouched in the attic as floodwaters rise, huddled in the basement as tornadoes pass over, hidden in a foxhole on the battlefield, cowering behind locked doors in a classroom as a gunman comes down the hall, people kneel together. I am always moved by this basic instinct in humanity. And when we look at the neurobiology in trauma, we find something even more remarkable about this behavior.

Prayer is a key element in most spiritual and religious practices, and even those who do not profess to a religious tradition describe praying in times of acute danger or stress. During prayer, the body relaxes and the autonomic system becomes more efficient. One researcher reports, "Acute physiological changes occurring during prayer and meditation have been extensively researched and show a reduction of sympathetic nervous system activity."[8] Prayer decreases autonomic fight/flight/freeze responses.

Deep breathing that naturally occurs during prayer can assist the body's parasympathetic nervous system during its recovery process. Throughout the day, it can serve as a nervous system reset button. Perhaps it takes the form of a grandmother's frequent rosary, a table grace before a meal, a pastor's prayer before starting a workday, or a silent meditation early in the morning and again just before bed. The Muslim Salat prayer takes place five times each day, with set patterns and words, offered in a right spirit and directly raised up to God. Using electroencephalography, researchers have found that during Salat, "parasympathetic activity increased, and sympathetic activity decreased."[9]

Prayers in many traditions include set patterns and repeated phrases. When these prayers are offered during calm states, the body learns how to re-create a similar relaxation state even in new or threatening circumstances. Whether rote or spontaneous, prayers are powerful tools against daily fear and anxiety and increase our ability to stay calm and act wisely during trauma. Familiar prayers, mantras, and chants spoken aloud provide a way to bring a worried mind back to the present moment.

Breathing deeply, we alert our brains to release tension and begin to feel that all is (or soon will be) well again. Daily prayer practice helps us access this physiological shift at any time. Faith community prayers can help members increase their stress tolerance. If everyone understood how vital the prayer time is during worship, they would stretch it out, allowing more silence and spending more time in prayer whenever they gathered.

Let me illustrate the power within prayer from your body's perspective. A chaplain I'll call Manny was the only person allowed to hold the hand of a seventy-year-old Covid-19 patient as he died. Having noted the man's denominational affiliation, Manny offered traditional prayers. But as the man drew closer to death, Manny's prayers grew quieter and simpler. At the last all he could say was, "It'll be okay. . . . It'll be okay. . . . It'll be okay," which he repeated like a chant. He took a long breath in, and on the out breath, like a sigh, he said again, "It'll be okay."

Afterward, reflecting on this moment, he wondered if he had said the right things and why he chose "it'll be okay" as his last prayer with the man, because by all rational analysis, the circumstance was not at all okay; it was terribly wrong. The man had no time to prepare for his death, no family with him, no chance to be held by people he loved. He had only a stranger to reassure him. "Eventually I figured it out," Manny told a colleague. "God directed me to those words because *I* needed them—so that I could stay with the man when my body wanted to run, my spirit wanted to rail at every aspect of pandemic injustice, and my grief for his family was overwhelming." Manny was experiencing the man's traumatic death too, feeling powerless as the lone witness to the man's suffering. His secondary trauma was very real, and to stay in the acute care isolation room, he had to fight against his bodily alert system, which is why that prayer showed up. A long deep breath in and an audible breath out awakened his parasympathetic nervous system and connected his brain to dopamine receptors, which sent signals informing him that all was, in fact, okay. Manny was not in danger, but his body thought otherwise! And so, he prayed.

Research from diverse spiritual practices indicates that many forms of prayer are effective. Manny needn't have worried about the words he used; the act of praying was sufficient. Most chaplains and many clergy know that prayer releases fear as death nears, and we have prayed as beloved souls entered into eternity. Words, chants, and silence can all bring calm. Alone or in a group, the words we say to ourselves or words someone else says on our behalf all contribute to mental and physical well-being. People affiliated with faith-based organizations who learn to pray and practice prayer improve their overall well-being. Prayer prepares us for life and for death.

THE HEALING GIFT OF CONNECTION

My grandmother was the ad hoc spiritual director in our family. When I was in high school, we'd sit by her front window at a little table covered with a crocheted doily. Her worn leather Bible lay open to selected verses she wanted to share with me, and next to it she'd have a small vase with a single flower. After a little check-in time, she'd share Bible verses with me that she had highlighted with a marker. When I was anxious, she chose just the right text to reassure me. When things in the family looked rocky and conflicted, rather than delve into the problems, my grandmother affirmed the love we shared, reinforcing our connection. As my parents' marriage disintegrated, it was my grandmother who shored up my fear that they'd leave each other and abandon me by telling me that underneath it all, they were still deeply and loyally in love. While I go about my work to restore attachment wounds during trauma care, I often think about my grandmother's ability to see and name Divine love and human love in action.

Hearing Scripture verses read aloud can be a lifeline for those who have relied on them for many years, as precious as the first words we hear a nurse speak to us as we come up from anesthesia in the recovery room. They connect us with the Divine within us and beyond us. As clergy, many of us have seen the way reading Psalm 22, offering the Lord's prayer, or saying the Mi Shebeirach prayer for healing brings physical as well as mental comfort to patients in the hospital, particularly as death draws near. These sacred moments demand the best of us. We rely on our faith traditions, Scripture verses and prayers we memorize and recite, and our comfort with silence to calm fear and reduce trauma.

During and after trauma, chaplains, clergy, and spiritual directors help survivors strengthen their attachment to God (or other named sources of life and strength) as a way to restore hope and healing. They choose Scripture passages that affirm connection. "Nothing can ever separate us from God's love" (Rom 8:38 NLT) is on a playlist I run in my head when I'm overwhelmed. Familiar verses connect us to God, and they remind us that we are not alone.

Therapists call a loving relationship between human beings an attachment. Pastoral counselors and spiritual directors believe that a Divine-human relationship also provides a vital emotional attachment. A spiritual attachment can be as strong as—or stronger than—any human relationship. Scripture and prayers emphasizing the presence of the Holy Spirit, Christ, or God strengthen this relationship.

I believe that connecting congregants to the Divine is at the core of pastoral work. Trauma destroys trust and attachment, especially when primary attachment figures are abusive or have died. Since humans thrive on close connection, clergy are gifted with many opportunities to foster and reinforce healthy spiritual attachment. To assist trauma victims, trauma-informed clergy use prayer and Scriptures to help them move from Divine and human disengagement to reengagement. They may need to feel safely connected to a holy presence before they begin to reach out for human hands to hold.

While powerful Bible passages and familiar prayers may offer hope and healing, they can also be roadblocks. Caring for brokenhearted people, trauma-informed clergy let victims/survivors lead the way. Words can harm as well as heal. I once asked a client who was going through a terrible divorce after her husband's infidelity if she found it helpful to meditate or pray. She was silent. "I don't pray these days," she said. "I can't figure out what to call God. My father was abusive, so I don't use that. The word *Lord* has never worked for me. I'm finally getting free from someone who has been lording it over me for years. I don't need that!" I nodded, paused, and took a few deep breaths. "What if you called God by what you need?" She quickly smiled and responded, "I'd start my prayer, 'Oh, Non-abandoning One.'" So this is how she began to pray again. Drawing strength from her restored relationship with her non-abandoning One, she found her way to new life.

This wise woman taught me to stop before I offer a prayer and ask two questions: "By what name do you invoke God or Spirit?"

and "What do you want me to pray for?" By asking these questions, I get myself out of the way. Each victim/survivor has a unique relationship with the Divine, which may or may not have anything in common with mine.

Our job as trauma-informed clergy is to be honest after faith-shaking, or faith-destroying life experiences. We affirm that every spiritual relationship, like every human relationship, changes. It goes through periods of disconnection (anger, sadness, and loneliness) as well as close connection (warmth, tenderness, and safety). We are in a unique position from which to help victims repair spiritual relationships. If their prior beliefs were utterly destroyed by violence, abuse, or grief—we join them in their search for new ones. By our willingness to witness great suffering, we also witness miracles as victims move from powerlessness to empowerment and from isolation to connection.

CHAPTER ELEVEN
TRAUMA RECOVERY STAGES
VICTIM, SURVIVOR, THRIVER

Healing and restoring God, give me patience when the journey to wellness takes its good old time. Reveal yourself along the way. I am often as clueless as Jesus's disciples were on the day when he walked and talked with them after his resurrection. Some days, I just don't recognize you, and yet you break bread with me, you open my heart to connect with you, you promise never-ending comfort. Other days, I see your power when green grass emerges from a fire-scorched valley, when the world faces down a deadly disease, and when prophets cry out for change. After every violence, tragedy, or loss, you are all about resurrection. Selah.

On a tour with Southern Oregon Land Conservancy, a small group of hikers went up to a high valley along the Cascade Mountain range one early June. With permission from landowners whose property they traversed, they followed a wooded path to the edge of an open meadow. Their guide stopped the group and asked them to describe what they saw before them. It was an expansive vista of late spring wildflowers, butterfly-loving milkweed, yellow mules' ears, purple native iris, tall grasses quivering in a light breeze, and a flyover by a red-winged blackbird. The guide smiled and urged the group forward. What happened next unnerved them. They stepped from volcanic rock and hard packed dirt onto the spongy surface of a rare, forty-acre wetland that felt like an extrafirm waterbed. With each step, they felt the ground give slightly, and though it held them up, they could see undulating ripples flow away from them in the vegetation. At first, they all instinctively froze in place and became silent. They'd been onboard boats listing from side to side, but this was much less solid. They were walking on a meadow fed by mineral-rich springs covered over by several feet of matted vegetation. Life was growing beneath the surface that couldn't have survived above ground. With each sloshy step, they couldn't be sure if the surface would hold or if their feet would plunge into water. It was unlike anything they had ever experienced. While the ground looked solid, it wasn't. The hikers found it confusing at first, and they had to slow down to let their bodies rebalance and then make adjustments. It was truly a hike unlike any they had ever taken.

A walk through the quaking fen is an apt description of life after trauma. Things may look "normal" but definitely are not. Solid ground gives way, replaced by an emotionally unstable landscape. There's a lot going on under the surface. Trauma survivors must learn to live with uncertainty, slow down and rebalance, muster great courage, and then trust themselves to walk forward.

GROWTH STAGES IN RECOVERY

After trauma, three growth stages emerge: victim, survivor, thriver. In ministry, we don't just drop into a victim's life for a once-and-done debriefing. We accompany them for days, months, maybe years. This gives us the chance to see their healing trajectory. We notice the words individuals use to describe themselves along the way. Do they only use the word *victim* initially or use it for a long while? When do they start calling themselves *survivors*? As recovery continues, their self-image and self-efficacy change, and picking up on these verbal signposts can be very helpful. A man who had been held at gunpoint during a robbery described his recovery like this: "I used to ask, 'Why me?' but now I ask, 'Why not me?'" Notice the way his self-perception was changing. As victims move forward in healing, they begin to tell the story of what happened to them differently, perhaps with fewer details or less intensity.

Where once the traumatic event was the whole story, it may become one part of a larger narrative. What is the rest of the story? Facts and details begin to be less important than the meaning ascribed to them.

As victims reframe their life stories after trauma, the process may be very quick or painfully slow. These stages may overlap or circle back around. While we accompany wounded ones, we listen for their self-perceptions and meaning-making narratives. We can then promote healing by providing feedback that validates growth.

Stage One: Victim

The victim stage is marked by enormous suffering. Cognitive, emotional, and physical symptoms last from one to three months and may fall within the diagnostic parameters for PTSD. Beyond six months, the condition is diagnosed as either chronic (long-term) or complex (indicating multiple traumas or the presence of overlapping conditions, such as depression or anxiety).

During this first stage, people feel powerless and disconnected. They typically aren't ready to interpret what just happened. Going through the motions of daily living can be challenging, and they need others to help them. They may turn to a spouse or friend to nudge them out of bed, take them for a walk, or share a meal. Or they may be so crushed that they isolate themselves and refuse help.

Intense physiological symptoms are dominant in this stage. A woman who had three car crashes within a year said, "I feel like there's a bull's-eye on the side of my car." After the third accident, when she tried getting into the driver's seat of her SUV, her legs buckled. Her sleep was disturbed by nightmares. She was distracted at work and withdrawn at home. Her body was clearly in charge during this part of her healing process.

Victims in this phase feel stuck, helpless, and out of control. They are quickly overwhelmed by strong emotions. Their previous coping mechanisms don't do the job of clearing away the pain. Even with supportive family members and friends, they often feel terribly alone. Suffering can lead to hopelessness, and hopelessness may lead to suicidal thoughts and feelings.

Ways to Help Victims

To care for victims in this early stage, help them build support networks. Encourage them to stay in daily contact with loved ones and dear ones and to accept help. Offer referrals (and co-pays, if needed) to trauma-informed therapists. When victims describe their symptoms in this early stage, listen carefully. If they describe a great deal of sadness or pain, don't be afraid to ask, "Do you ever think about ending your life?" If they say yes and have a plan, or if they don't think they could stop themselves, call a suicide hotline or take them to the nearest hospital emergency room.

As I noted early in the book, more than 80 percent of people recover from a single traumatic event without developing ongoing symptoms. Some of them never identify themselves as "victims." But for a few, particularly people with adverse childhood experiences or repeated traumas in adulthood, being a victim can become a fixed self-perception.

People can get stuck in this stage and become defined by a traumatic event they never recover from. In the field of psychology, we talk about the difference between a personality state and a personality trait. Trauma recovery may depend on this difference. Someone who has come to believe that they are and always will be a victim has a personality trait that will make recovery more difficult. Taking steps to recover, finding self-efficacy, and taking ownership of one's responses to the trauma all depend on personality. If "victim" is a trait, then it operates similarly in all circumstances—at home, at work, or in a faith community. For those who are fused with the victim identity, relationships are fraught with anxious distrust. They accuse others of ill intention, and minor slights seem like egregious emotional assaults.

States and Traits

"*States* are characteristic patterns of thinking, feeling, and behaving in a concrete situation at a specific moment in time. *Traits* are characteristic patterns of thinking, feeling, and behaving that generalize across similar situations, differ systematically between individuals, and remain rather stable across time."[1] States are more fluid, and they change over time and in different situations, whereas traits are fixed features that do not often change.

A concerned pastor referred Martina to my office for treatment. Martina had seen other therapists and described them as lacking empathy and expecting too much from her. Recently, she had verbally assaulted a male youth leader in the church parking lot for not doing enough to protect her daughter and other youth—for not giving them information about online sexual predation and date rape.

According to witnesses, the staff member stepped back from Martina as the conversation escalated, and onlookers gathered around to see what was happening. The youth leader asked her to please lower her voice and urged her to take a few breaths before saying anything more, since curious teens were now also listening. She then accused him of being unsafe around them too and told him that she would no longer permit her daughter to attend youth events.

The senior pastor learned about it before the day was out, and he invited Martina to his office the next day. She told him that the youth minister had provoked her and scared her. (She did not tell him that she was dealing with reawakened trauma.) She demanded a meeting with the board of directors at the church so she could ask them to fire the youth director. A kind group of lay leaders met with her but couldn't dispel her hostility. By then, she was angry at the senior minister, too, for having blamed her for being out of control rather than addressing the church "staff problem." The situation escalated when she made phone calls to church members telling them that the church wasn't an emotionally safe place and urged them to leave along with her. The next day, the senior pastor referred her to me. We were both surprised that she called for an appointment.

At our first session, she readily disclosed her life story and history of victimization. She grew up with a verbally abusive father and an emotionally closed off mother. At age seventeen, she enlisted in the army and moved away from the stress back home. Sadly, though, like far too many women in the armed services, she was raped by a senior officer.[2] She had the courage to report it, but he was not punished, and she was verbally reprimanded. She became increasingly depressed, and when she couldn't function any longer, she was discharged. This experience added to her perception that the world is totally unjust and unsafe—which was true for her in the military, but which she globalized. To feel more empowered, she took up the heroic job of lashing out at others to keep from becoming a victim again. She said, "I have my sword drawn and ready" for any threatening situation. With intensely damaged attachment and her trust in people destroyed, she developed an understandably inflexible identity trait. I suspected that it wouldn't be long in therapy until she came to believe that I too was failing to help her so she could keep her strongly held belief in her victimhood. At each session, I sat only a few feet away from her drawn sword. She would either lay down the sword as I gained her trust or reenact her victimization with me too.

When the Victim Becomes the Problem

In every organization there are members with trauma histories, as you have learned in this book. A small number of them are still acting out their unhealed trauma as antagonists or victims. Clergy and laity who study trauma can see and identify this underlying psychopathology. Caring congregants need to hold their boundaries tightly, and clergy need to avoid codependent behavior with a victim who is acting out. When unhealed people wreak emotional havoc by drawing attention to themselves or lashing out at others, their behavior must be stopped, and they need therapeutic interventions.

Having been victimized doesn't give anyone the right to monopolize the time of clergy, church leaders, and staff or to emotionally abuse them. In one particularly egregious circumstance, a congregation had to ask a member to leave, knowing full well that she would call herself an innocent victim of their actions. Afterward, she used social media to slander the pastor and the congregation, wrote graffiti on the church's front walkway where people would see it when they arrived at worship, and dissuaded community groups from holding events in the building. Her strong need to maintain her victim status could not be easily addressed and would never be satisfied.

Most victims do not get stuck in this place, but when they do, it helps to see whether the faith community or family and friends are offering them secondary rewards, such as enormous amounts of attention and pity, or a social network of fellow victim-sufferers. For people with fixed victim traits, the role of victim has advantages. They may . . .

- avoid taking responsibility for their trauma recovery
- lay their unhappiness at the feet of others
- bounce from one therapist to another and remain unsatisfied with treatment
- avoid making changes because they haven't done anything wrong
- feel morally superior to keep them from feeling powerless instead
- seek unending monetary support from family, friends, social services, and faith communities

After trauma, there are also disadvantages to staying in the victim role. A victim identity limits personal growth and prolongs feelings of helplessness. People in the victim role let others (or manipulate others to) control their behavior. Those who are stuck in the victim role may end up bringing anger and conflict into relationships with the very people who are trying to help them. When victims become extremely passive, other people are more likely to prey on their vulnerability. Complex psychological defenses are used by unhealthy people who get stuck in the victim role.

In any faith community, a story can be told about just such a member, leader, or staff person. Social psychologists observe a pattern they call victim-signaling among unhealed trauma survivors. These individuals draw attention to themselves by being more broken, more wounded, and more in need than other congregants. They may demand attention and try to get it in a negative way. These individuals can benefit from group therapy, especially a treatment known as dialectic behavior therapy (DBT), which includes working with an individual therapist who is "on call" for the client and group therapy where self-soothing and prosocial behaviors are examined and practiced.

Exploring Your Reactions

What can clergy do to help people when they exhibit victim behaviors? Start by noticing how unhealthy emotional dynamics affect you. Does someone you are trying to help leave you on edge, feeling drained, angry, or otherwise emotionally entangled? Take note of those feelings and trust them. If you say to someone, "So-and-so is making me crazy!" you might be right. Are you being drawn into emotional enmeshment with a very unhealthy person? If you find yourself thinking, "No matter what I do (or the faith community does), it's not enough," trust your inner wisdom. If your ego tells you that you are more skilled, insightful, and compassionate than other care providers, do not believe it. Recognize your limits, set boundaries, and step back for a while. Working with someone in the victim role is exhausting. It's a good time to reach out to a colleague or mental health provider for supervision.

Clergy leaders provide what is called carefrontation, which is confrontation done in a loving way. A carefrontation doesn't label a person; it labels a negative behavior. It avoids "should" and "must" and invites positive change. Asking a perpetual victim to look at and stop unhelpful behaviors creates a healthier faith community. Congregants and leaders can easily be drawn into victim-signaling behaviors, such as monopolization of a group, expressions of moral superiority, and distraction so that other programs and people are sidelined. Trauma-informed clergy are aware that these individuals wind up hurting themselves and damaging their faith communities. They encourage prosocial behaviors, and if they don't see change, pluck up the courage to ask the problematic congregant to leave the faith community.

Stage Two: Survivor

Most victims of trauma do not get stuck in the victim role and do not have a personality trait that interferes with recovery. In the next phase, most victims stop using that word and begin calling themselves survivors. This phase is all about recovery. A man who was attacked by his wife struggled to use the term *victim* even after the courts convicted her of assault. He didn't like the term; he felt shame for not being stronger and more capable of standing up for himself. He embraced the term *survivor* instead. He chose to move quickly to the second stage.

In the survivor phase, people shift from helplessness to hopefulness. They take more control over their lives. They can look after their own needs again. In my earlier story about my divorce, I illustrated this shift as it took place over time. I went from eating beef stew out of a can and drinking flat champagne to setting my table with fine china, buying myself flowers, and cooking nutritious meals.

Emotions become more stable and more manageable during this phase. Anger changes from a physical adrenal response to more rational thinking that can be delved into or released. Sadness changes too. Tears come less often and flow for shorter periods. Laughter reappears. Optimism sneaks in.

In this phase, right-brain memories of the trauma can more easily be transferred into left-brain storage, where logic, storytelling, and mental reasoning live. Emotional memories of the traumatic moments start to "make sense" rather than overwhelm survivors. Spiritual questions and quests begin. The survivor can begin to experience solace.

Survivors return to work and leisure activities. Their self-care increases. This is a good time for them to take up something new, such as meditation, yoga, writing, or learning to play an instrument. Many survivors explore ways to further their education. They begin to invest in new relationships or reinvest in old ones. They make plans for the future but may not take concrete steps to achieve them yet. They may be "back on their feet" again, go to therapy, and increase self-care. But they are also still fragile and can be easily retraumatized or emotionally reinjured. They may return to old patterns that were harmful or dysfunctional before the trauma, and people who

care about them can notice and name these patterns in order to help
them stay on track.

Ways to Help Survivors

In this recovery stage, let the survivor lead the way. Restore their power
by letting them reframe their story and start to claim a fuller identity.
Coping skills that were offline during phase one are now back on board.
Ask them, "How have you survived other devastating times in your
life?" and help them to look back on skills, talents, and resources that
helped them through. What soothes them when the pain returns? What
keeps their anxiety at bay? Asking them what works will reinforce those
coping mechanisms.

Cultural bias may operate during recovery. Internalized racism and
gender bias can negatively affect a survivor's viewpoint. Survivors
ask, "How can I live a full and happy life again?" People around them
may set overt or covert limits for them. Sometimes, other people will
co-opt a victim by limiting them with comments like "You'll never
amount to anything," or, with egocentric altruism, "I can help you rise
beyond your place (station)." This is particularly insidious for BIPOC
survivors, who may have internalized race- and class-biased pressures
to stay in the victim role. Class-dominant White people may take
credit for lifting them up to a higher caste and opening doors to their
achievement. This is the Henry Higgins and Eliza Doolittle narrative,
which is overtly racist, classist, and misogynistic.

High school senior Elijah Megginson, in an opinion article about his
college application essay, wrote about feeling pressured to describe
his trauma history. He was repeatedly told by mentors that he should
highlight his terrible childhood to increase his chances of college
admission and scholarships. The more misery he could describe, the
more his "overachievement" would open doors for him. He wisely
resisted. Megginson wrote, "Trauma is one of life's teachers. We are
molded by it, and some will choose to write about it urgently, pas-
sionately. Yet I would encourage those who feel like their stories were

written in tragedy to rethink that, as I did. When you open your mind to all the other things you can offer in life, it becomes liberating."[3] By refusing to be seen as a model survivor—perpetually seen as a victim or an exceptional minority—he claimed and named his strengths.

Stage Three: Thriver

In the thriver stage, people acknowledge their trauma. They have experienced great pain, but they choose to no longer be defined by it. Thrivers are ready to claim new identities and begin new lives. They have put the once-shattered pieces of their lives back together and are now ready for positive and prosocial actions. They may change jobs, have a baby, or begin a degree program. They may uproot and move to a new community so their identity as victim no longer predominates, especially if the story of their trauma was extremely public. They may leave behind a supportive community or faith community, wanting to be known for their new life rather than their damaged old one. They settle into new identities.

I frequently ask clergy who take my courses on trauma-informed care, Were you called to ministry in the midst of a personal or family trauma? A majority say yes. This group of thrivers has a unique call to better the world, and they are uniquely skilled at caring for their congregants during and following trauma. They speak about scriptural themes within the Passover and Easter narratives from their firsthand experience with liberation, healing, and new life.

Thriver Consciousness

Spend a few minutes breathing deeply and raising up gratitude for your ability to reinvent yourself after pain and suffering. Have you gone from victim to survivor to thriver? Thank your nervous system for protecting you and teaching you the difference between an emergency and a false alarm. Thank the rest of your body for getting your attention, giving you strength when needed, and healing you. Thank your emotions for drawing you down

> *into dark loneliness and pulling you up again. Thank your brain for organizing your past and giving you language and story. Lift up thanks for friends who have assisted you along the way. Praise Spirit, Creator, Guide, Light, Wisdom. Lift your holy hands and offer praise for your resurrection!*

Thrivers go on to help others, create movements, and work toward a less violent, safer world. Thrivers are ready to address trauma through justice seeking. This is the time when abuse victims confront their abusers, when people wounded by faith communities challenge past complicity.

A man in his late fifties spent three years in therapy facing his pain and working through lifelong patterns that flowed from his prior sexual abuse. And in the process, he decided to confront the faith community and denomination wherein he was molested and abused as a teen. The confrontation itself retraumatized him, but it did not stop him. He took legal action against the denomination and won. And then, in the year after he won his financial settlement, he used those funds to "pay" himself so he could work with statewide organizations to prevent child sexual abuse. His work included supporting legislative action to remove statutes of limitation, speaking publicly, writing a book, supporting other victims (including less visible male victims), and advocating for victim rights.[4]

Like this man, other victims have become survivors and then, as thrivers, started justice movements. There are thousands of them, including #MeToo and Mothers Against Drunk Driving. Two moms whose sons died in fraternity hazings after they were forced to drink excessively, formed the Antihazing Coalition. March for Our Lives is an organization dedicated to ending gun violence that was formed by victims/survivors of the Parkland, Florida, school shooting. Many of these movements receive financial and volunteer help from faith communities. They are made up of people who have been touched by traumatic grief and allies who join the cause.

Possibly the best known of these movements is the Black Lives Matter movement. Essayists Julian DeShazier and Damon A. Williams, in their book *Spiritual Care in an Age of #BlackLivesMatter*, write about helpful and harmful church responses to movements for justice. They note that the task of faith communities who care for victims is to take up antiviolence: "Antiviolence is intentional action to reduce and prevent harm, provide benefit, and protect from violence. . . . [It] is the ethical commitment to harm no person, mixed with the existential commitment to stop one's own or another person's harm."[5] Many thriver-formed groups carry this ethic into their work and teach faith-based organizations how to do the same. The teachers are showing up, and we can make our communities safer and stronger by listening, reading, observing, and joining thrivers in action.

Ways to Help Thrivers

In pastoral care, you have the honor and privilege to observe a thriver in a period of transformative healing. At this stage, pastoral care is more responsive and less directive. Obstacles that were once insurmountable have become invigorating challenges. Your job is to offer affirmation, remain available if/as needed, and encourage and support thrivers in their new endeavors. When justice work becomes their "call," you can gather the power and resources within the faith community to stand with them as advocates for social change.

TRANSFORMATION

I have been blessed to witness radical healing transformations after trauma. Some have been bold and public, but many subtle, quiet, spiritual experiences also occur during recovery. In the classic children's story *The Secret Garden*, Archibald Craven is a widower in deep intractable pain for nearly a dozen years. His wife died giving birth to his son, who doctors feared was gravely ill and confined to his room. Archibald was not allowed to see or touch the boy. Author Frances Hodgson Burnett describes him as a man the light "had never seemed to touch," until one day while sitting by a gentle river, grieving over his dead wife and crippled son, something shifted ever so slightly.

He found himself "looking as he remembered he had looked at such things years ago. . . . It was as if a sweet clear spring had begun to rise in a stagnant pool and had risen and risen until at last it swept the dark water away." The experience rattled Archibald. "'What is it?'" he said, almost in a whisper, and he passed his hand over his forehead. "'I almost feel as if—I were alive!'"

The story's narrator aptly describes healing's subtle mysteries as the book's main characters all move from victims to survivors to thrivers. She admits to her astonishment when Archibald comes alive again: "I do not know enough about the wonderfulness of undiscovered things to be able to explain how this had happened to him. Neither does anyone else yet. He did not understand at all himself."[6] When I ask survivors how they did it—how they overcame, how they healed—many of them talk about their healing in existential terms. Growth is mysterious and wondrous.

In Paul's Epistle to the Hebrews, he writes about people overcoming obstacles, finding their way out of slavery and oppression, sometimes giving God praise and sometimes in angry defiance along the way. He notes that by faith "what is seen was made from things that are not visible" (Heb 11:3). Those on Paul's "Who's Who" list of faithful people included victims, survivors, and thrivers. By faith they overcame, received power, gave birth, lived in solidarity with foreigners. One of them sent her baby downriver in a basket, praying for his rescue. They were a mixed lot, both the oppressed and oppressors. Society's outcasts and honored citizens. They trusted and they doubted. Some of them obeyed, and some rebelled. They made the journey by faith. But whose faith? Their faith in God or God's faith in them? God believed in them more than many of them believed in God. By faith, God liberated and saved them. God trusted them to heal. This is the job we have as trauma-informed clergy. We trust them to heal.

Belief in miracles lightens the burdens of trauma care. As you do this work, you may sometimes wonder if you are helping or hurting. You may take someone's suffering home in the evening or awaken with anxiety or sadness in the middle of the night. You may feel like giving up, just like victims do. You will be forced to explore your own trauma and be sure that you are healing it. It is hard work, but you are not alone. As you come alongside very wounded people, please reach out to colleagues, a therapist, a spiritual director, and trusted friends. The Non-abandoning One, the Creator and Re-creator, the one who brings green shoots from dead tree stumps and leads us from every dark tomb, this God has faith in you.

ACKNOWLEDGMENTS

I was prompted to write this book amid three traumatic experiences: a pandemic, a fire, and a racially charged homicide in my community. Teaching chaplains and clergy across the country how to respond in similar traumatic conditions led to the development of this content. I have written this book for clergy and lay ministers everywhere who have compassionate hearts and the courage to stand alongside victims during and after trauma.

My heartfelt gratitude goes out to my three clergy sisters, Beth Gaede, Yolanda Villa, and Pamela Nelson-Munson, for their collaboration and care-filled reading during the shaping of this book. We share God's call to heal the world through writing and pastoral care, and we offer this book to our colleagues, believing that competent clergy and faith communities repair trauma by offering safety, healing, and justice.

NOTES

Chapter One

1 I have chosen to follow current American Psychological Association publication practices and refer to racial categories for people in this book with capital letters. While this decision is controversial, my aim is to challenge the presumption that lowercase "white" is the norm. Skin color nomenclature was invented (with biblical justifications) to reinforce insidious social ranking in the late eighteenth century. Any classification system that prejudicially separates people needs reconsideration.

2 This data is from Richard A. Oppel Jr., Robert Gebeloff, K. K. Rebecca Lai, Will Wright, and Mitch Smith, "The Fullest Look Yet at the Racial Inequity of Coronavirus," *New York Times*, July 5, 2020, https://www.nytimes.com/interactive/2020/07/05/us/coronavirus-latinos-african-americans-cdc-data.html?action=click&action=click&pgtype=Article&state=default&module=styln-coronavirus&variant=1_show&region=MAIN_CONTENT_1&context=STYLN_TOP_LINKS_recirc&module=RelatedLinks&pgtype=Article.

Chapter Two

1 Adapted from the University of Buffalo Center for Social Research, "What Is Trauma-Informed Care?," accessed May 20, 2021, http://socialwork.buffalo.edu/social-research/institutes-centers/institute-on-trauma-and-trauma-informed-care/what-is-trauma-informed-care.html.

2 James Baldwin, "Stranger in the Village," in *Notes of a Native Son* (Boston: Beacon, 2012), 163.

3 To describe Chaplain Kibben's experience, I am drawing on the account by Jack Jenkins, "How House Chaplain Calmed Tense Hours in Besieged Capitol with Prayers for 'God's Covering,'" *Religion News Service*, January 9, 2021, https://religionnews.com/2021/01/09/house-chaplain-siege/.

4 Jenkins.

5 The fields of psychology, neuroscience, and theology combine in a new field, founded by Dr. Andrew Newburg and described in his book *Principles of Neurotheology* (New York: Routledge, 2016), which includes his research on the brain-changing effects of daily meditation and prayer. You might also want to read Rick

Hanson's book, *Buddha's Brain: The Practical Neuroscience of Happiness, Love, and Wisdom* (Oakland, CA: New Harbinger, 2009).

6 "Sen. Patty Murray Recounts Her Narrow Escape from a Violent Mob inside the U.S. Capitol," PBS News Hour, February 12, 2021, https://www.pbs.org/newshour/show/sen-patty-murray-recounts-her-narrow-escape-from-a-violent-mob-inside-the-u-s-capitol.

7 Resmaa Menakem, *My Grandmother's Hands: Racialized Trauma and the Pathway to Mending Our Hearts and Bodies* (Las Vegas: Central Recovery, 2017).

Chapter Three

1 To read more about my father's life, I invite you to read my memoir, Karen McClintock, *My Father's Closet* (Columbus: Ohio State University Press, 2017).

2 Dr. Joy DeGruy, "Post Traumatic Slave Syndrome," accessed February 24, 2021, https://www.joydegruy.com/post-traumatic-slave-syndrome.

3 Karen McClintock, *When Trauma Wounds: Pathways to Healing and Hope* (Minneapolis: Fortress, 2019).

4 Deb Dana, *The Polyvagal Theory in Therapy: Engaging the Rhythm of Regulation* (New York: W. W. Norton, 2018).

5 American Psychiatric Association, *Diagnostic and Statistical Manual of Mental Disorders (DSM-5)*, 5th ed. (Washington, DC: APA, 2013), 271, 272.

6 American Psychiatric Association, 277.

Chapter Four

1 American Psychiatric Association, *DSM-5*, 790.

2 American Psychiatric Association, 789–90.

3 Ann W. Nguyen, "Religion and Mental Health in Racial and Ethnic Minority Populations: A Review of Literature," *Innovation in Aging* 4, no. 5 (August 2020): 1, https://doi.org/10.1093/geroni/igaa035.

4 Stephanie Jordan, "When African Americans Grieve," Fuller Life Family Therapy Institute, October 19, 2020, https://fullerlifefamilytherapy.org/when-african-americans-grieve/.

5 Nguyen, "Religion and Mental Health," 6.

6 Tom Gjelten, "Clergy on the Pandemic Front Lines: 'How Do We Really Grieve?,'" interview by Tom Gjelten, *All Things Considered*, NPR, February 22, 2021, audio, 4:01, https://www.npr.org/2021/02/22/969225381/clergy-on-the-pandemic-front-lines-how-do-we-really-grieve.

7 Corina Knoll, Ali Watkins, and Michael Rothfeld, "'I Couldn't Do Anything': The Virus and an E.R. Doctor's Suicide," *New York Times*, July 11, 2020, https://www.nytimes.com/2020/07/11/nyregion/lorna-breen-suicide-coronavirus.html.

8 Matthew W. Gallagher et al., "Examining Associations between Covid-19 Experiences and Post Traumatic Stress," *Journal of Loss and Trauma*, February 17, 2021, https://doi.org/10.1080/15325024.2021.1886799.

9 Kelsie Smith, "Couple Married for 70 Years Dies from Covid-19 Simply Days Earlier Than Appointment to Get Vaccine," CNN, January 22, 2021, https://www.cnn.com/2021/01/22/us/a-couple-married-70-years-dies-of-covid-trnd/index.html.

Chapter Five

1 Dan Bates, "The 4 Tasks of Grieving," *Psychology Today*, November 8, 2019, https://www.psychologytoday.com/us/blog/mental-health-nerd/201911/the-4-tasks-grieving.

2 Emily Hernandez, Aracely Rosales, and Martin Brodwin, "Death and Dying Latino/a Cultural View of Death," California Association for Postsecondary Education and Disability, 2018, http://www.caped.io/fall-2018/death-and-dying-latino-a-cultural-view-of-death/.

3 Marilyn A. Mendoza, "Death and Bereavement among the Lakota," *Psychology Today*, October 7, 2017, https://www.psychologytoday.com/us/blog/understanding-grief/201710/death-and-bereavement-among-the-lakota.

4 Maria Yellow Horse Brave Heart, "Historical Trauma and Unresolved Grief: Implications for Clinical Research and Practice with Indigenous Peoples of the Americas" (PhD diss., University of New Mexico, 2017), https://www.ihs.gov/sites/telebehavioral/themes/responsive2017/display_objects/documents/slides/historicaltrauma/historicaltraumaintro0113.pdf. Maria is president of the Takini Institute, devoted to the healing of Native American and Indigenous trauma survivors.

5 Oppel Jr. et al., "Fullest Look Yet."

6 Claudia Rankine, as quoted in James Peterson, "The Color of Coronavirus: Our Mournful Undertaking," *Philadelphia Citizen*, June 18, 2020, https://thephiladelphiacitizen.org/black-mourning-during-covid/.

7 Learn more about Tonglen by watching videos and reading books by American nun, author, and teacher Pema Chodron.

8 American Heart Association, "How Churches Can Help during the Pandemic," April 21, 2020, https://www.heart.org/en/news/2020/04/21/how-churches-can-help-during-the-pandemic.

9 Cheryl Forster, "Intercultural Communication for Effective Diversity Work" (lecture, Mental Health Resource Network, Medford, OR, March 13, 2020).

10 Howard Thurman, "For a Time of Sorrow," in *Meditations of the Heart* (Boston: Beacon, 2014), 211–12. Used with permission from the Howard Thurman estate.

Chapter Six

1 Ali Mostafavi, "Hurricanes and Wildfires Are Colliding with the Covid-19 Pandemic—and Compounding the Risks," Conversation, August 27, 2020, https://theconversation.com/hurricanes-and-wildfires-are-colliding-with-the-covid-19-pandemic-and-compounding-the-risks-145003.

2 Anna Griffin, "An Exceptional Year, or the New Normal? A Pandemic. Protests. And Then the State Caught Fire," Oregon Public Broadcasting, December 31, 2020, https://www.opb.org/article/2020/12/31/an-exceptional-year-or-the-new-normal-a-pandemic-protests-and-then-the-state-caught-fire/.

3 A good long-term study about the aftermath in fire-ravaged communities is available in Vincent I. O. Agyapong et al., "Prevalence Rates and Predictors of Generalized Anxiety Disorder Symptoms in Residents of Fort McMurray Six Months after a Wildfire," *Frontiers in Psychiatry*, July 31, 2018, https://doi.org/10.3389/fpsyt.2018.00345.

4 Samantha Schmidt, "Wildfires Decimate Oregon Latino Community," *Washington Post*, September 10, 2020, https://www.washingtonpost.com/nation/2020/09/10/wildfires-decimate-oregon-latino-community/.

5 April Ehrlich, "FEMA Denied Most Oregon Requests for Wildfire Assistance," Oregon Public Broadcasting, February 11, 2021, https://www.opb.org/article/2021/02/11/oregon-2020-wildfires-fema-disaster-aid-denied/.

6 On February 14, 2021, the federal government issued an executive order, "to assist in organizing more effective efforts to serve people in need across the country and around the world, in partnership with civil society, including faith-based organizations." Joseph R. Biden Jr., "Executive Order on the Establishment of the White House Office of Faith-Based and Neighborhood Partnerships," White House, February 14, 2021, https://www.whitehouse.gov/briefing-room/presidential-actions/2021/02/14/executive-order-on-the-establishment-of-the-white-house-office-of-faith-based-and-neighborhood-partnerships/.

7 Referrals to trauma-informed providers are best when clergy have met and screened them ahead of time. Look for trauma-informed and culturally diverse therapists in your area. Even saying, "I can send you to a professional therapist" might be a roadblock for some people. Giving one or two names of therapists you have spoken with and trust will be most helpful.

8 SAMHSA, *Greater Impact: How Disasters Affect People of Low Socioeconomic Status*, Supplemental Research Bulletin (Rockville, MD: Disaster Technical Assistance Center, 2017), 3, 12, https://www.samhsa.gov/sites/default/files/dtac/srb-low-ses_2.pdf.

9 Ethan J. Raker et al., "Mitigating the Disparities after Natural Disasters: Lessons from the RISK Project," *Health Affairs* 39, no. 12 (December 2020), https://www.healthaffairs.org/doi/10.1377/hlthaff.2020.01161.

10 Matt 25:40.

Chapter Seven

1 The Indian Removal Act of 1830 forced the Cherokee, Chickasaw, Choctaw, Creek, and Seminole nations from their ancestral homes and relocated them to "Indian Territory," which basically covered the area that is now Oklahoma. To read more about past and present history, see Dwanna L. McKay's post, "Oklahoma Is—and Always Has Been—Native Land," Conversation, July 16, 2020, https://theconversation.com/oklahoma-is-and-always-has-been-native-land-142546.

2 Wikipedia, s.v. "Steal Away," last modified July 10, 2021, 23:20, https://en.wikipedia.org/wiki/Steal_Away.

3 Afri A. Atiba, "Rethinking Interpretive Tools for a Liberating Spiritual Care," in *Spiritual Care in an Age of #BlackLivesMatter: Examining the Spiritual and Prophetic Needs of African Americans in a Violent America*, ed. Danielle J. Buhuro (Eugene, OR: Cascade, 2019), 74.

4 "Underground Railroad Secret Codes," Harriet Tubman Historical Society, accessed July 4, 2021, http://www.harriet-tubman.org/underground-railroad-secret-codes/.

5 Katie Shepherd, "A Black Teen Was Fatally Shot in Oregon after Dispute over Loud Music, Police Say," *Seattle Times*, November 30, 2020, https://www.seattletimes.com/seattle-news/a-black-teen-was-fatally-shot-following-a-dispute-over-loud-music-police-say/.

6 Jayati Ramakrishnan, "Ashland Man Charged with Murder after Allegedly Shooting a 19-Year-Old Black Man over Loud Music," *Oregonian*, November 26, 2020, https://www.oregonlive.com/crime/2020/11/ashland-man-charged-with-murder-after-allegedly-shooting-a-19-year-old-black-man-over-loud-music.html.

7 According to the US Census Bureau, on July 1, 2019, 1.0 percent of Jackson County residents identified as Black. US Census Bureau, "Quick Facts: Jackson County, Oregon," accessed August 16, 2021, https://www.census.gov/quickfacts/fact/table/jacksoncountyoregon/PST045219.

8 Lillian Comas-Dias, Gordon Nagayama Hall, and Helen A. Neville, "Racial Trauma: Theory, Research, and Healing: Introduction to the Special Issue," *American Psychologist* 74, no. 1 (2019): 1.

9 Menakem, *Grandmother's Hands*, 9.

10 Menakem, 90.

11 Kelly Brown Douglas, *Sexuality and the Black Church: A Womanist Perspective* (New York: Orbis, 1999).

12 Ayumu Kaneko, "The Politics of the Black Rapist Myth: American Racial Violence, Gender and Class at the Turn of the 20th Century," *Jenda Shigaku* 3 (2007): 5–18.

13 See also Terrie M. Williams, *Black Pain: It Just Looks like We're Not Hurting* (New York: Scribner, 2008).

14 Menakem, *Grandmother's Hands*, 9.

15   Menakem, 37.

16   Erin D. Chapman, "Inciting an American Radicalism: The Sign in Sidney Bru-
     stein's Window and Lorraine Hansberry's Politics of Revolutionary Dissent" (pre-
     sentation, American Historical Association, Washington, DC, January 4, 2020).

17   Wikipedia, s.v. "George Floyd Protests," last modified July 11, 2021, 12:45, https://
     en.wikipedia.org/wiki/George_Floyd_protests.

18   Ibram X. Kendi, *How to Be an Antiracist* (New York: One World, 2019), 230.

19   "Fast Facts about American Religion," Ford Institute for Religion Research,
     accessed August 4, 2021, http://hirr.hartsem.edu/research/fastfacts/fast_facts
     .html#numcong.

20   Dr. David G. Lewis, anthropologist, fully describes the history of First Nation
     genocide in Oregon. David G. Lewis, "Home," Quartux, accessed August 4, 2021,
     https://ndnhistoryresearch.com/.

21   Martin Luther King Jr., "Letter from Birmingham Jail," first distributed as a pam-
     phlet in August of 1963 and soon thereafter published in magazines like the
     Atlantic Monthly and *Christian Century*. Martin Luther King Jr., "Letter from Bir-
     mingham Jail," CSU Chico IEGE, August 1963, https://www.csuchico.edu/iege/
     _assets/documents/susi-letter-from-birmingham-jail.pdf, p. 5.

22   Alan Blinder and Kevin Sack, "Dylann Roof Addressing Court Offers No Apol-
     ogy or Explanation for Massacre," *New York Times*, January 4, 2017, https://www
     .nytimes.com/2017/01/04/us/dylann-roof-sentencing.html.

23   Esth 4:14.

Chapter Eight

1   Emily Scott, "Your Brain Won't Work as Well: Tips for Spiritual Leaders during
    Covid-19," Medium, March 27, 2020, https://medium.com/@emilyscott_89364/
    your-brain-wont-work-as-well-tips-for-spiritual-leaders-during-covid-19
    -30aa71576dc5.

2   Julian DeShazier and Damon A. Williams, "When the Movement Gives Back," in
    Danielle J. Buhuro, ed., *Spiritual Care*, 24.

3   Peter A. Levine, *Waking the Tiger: Healing Trauma* (Berkeley, CA: North Atlan-
    tic, 1997).

4   Adam Grafa, "Somatic Experiencing: A Body-Centered Approach to Treating
    PTSD," Lyn-Lake Psychotherapy & Wellness, January 13, 2020, https://therapy
    -mn.com/somatic-experiencing-ptsd/.

5   Psychologist Francine Shapiro invented EMDR in the 1980s after noticing that
    moving her eyes from left to right rapidly reduced her own traumatic symptoms.

6   Donna Bach et al., "Clinical EFT (Emotional Freedom Techniques) Improves Multi-
    ple Physiological Markers of Health," *Journal of Evidence-Based Integrative Medicine*,
    February 19, 2019, https://www.ncbi.nlm.nih.gov/pmc/articles/PMC6381429/.

7 Bach et al.

8 Bessel Van Der Kolk, *The Body Keeps the Score: Brain, Mind, and Body in the Healing of Trauma* (New York: Penguin, 2014).

9 Jessica Schaffer, "TRE®: Tension and Trauma Releasing Exercises, an Introduction with Jessica Schaffer," Jessica Schaffer Nervous System RESET, January 15, 2015, YouTube video, 4:20, https://www.youtube.com/watch?v=67R974D8swM.

10 Stephen W. Porges, *The Polyvagal Theory: Neurophysiological Foundations of Emotions, Attachment, Communication, and Self-regulation* (New York: W. W. Norton, 2011).

11 Dana, *Polyvagal Theory*, 18–19.

12 Seth Porges, "The Polyvagal Theory: The New Science of Safety and Trauma," Nerd Nite, November 4, 2017, YouTube video, 28:09, https://youtu.be/br8-qebjIgs.

13 David Puder, "Episode 023: Emotional Shutdown—Understanding Polyvagal Theory," July 10, 2018, in *Psychiatry and Psychotherapy*, self-produced podcast, MP3 audio, 1:38:12, https://www.psychiatrypodcast.com/psychiatry-psychotherapy-podcast/polyvagal-theory-understanding-emotional-shutdown.

Chapter Nine

1 Lucian K. Truscott IV, "I'm a Direct Descendant of Thomas Jefferson. Take Down His Memorial," *New York Times*, June 6, 2020, https://www.nytimes.com/2020/07/06/opinion/thomas-jefferson-memorial-truscott.html?smid=em-share.

2 Stephanie Guerilus, "President Thomas Jefferson Descendant Wants His Statues Taken Down," theGrio, June 18, 2020, https://thegrio.com/2020/06/18/president-thomas-jefferson-descendant-statue/.

3 See also Exodus 20:5 and Deut 5:9.

4 William Shakespeare, *The Merchant of Venice*, act 3, sc. 5.

5 Shirley Ann Higuchi, *Setsuko's Secret: Heart Mountain and the Legacy of the Japanese American Incarceration* (Madison: University of Wisconsin Press, 2020).

6 Interviews with survivors and experts in these studies about Japanese American transgenerational trauma can be seen at Tom Ikeda, "Shirley Ann Higuchi: Setsuko's Secret," Ed Mays, December 31, 2020, YouTube video, 58:00, https://youtu.be/-v0Id41-kEw.

7 *Encyclopedia Britannica*, s.v. "Japanese American Internment," accessed April 16, 2021, https://www.britannica.com/event/Japanese-American-internment.

8 Densho is a grassroots organization, reference tool, and oral history center for the preservation, education, and storytelling of Japanese American World War II–era incarceration: https://densho.org/.

9 Judith Miller, "Wartime Internment of Japanese Was 'Grave Injustice,' Says Panel," *New York Times*, February 25, 1983, https://www.nytimes.com/1983/02/25/us/wartime-internment-of-japanese-was-grave-injustice-panel-says.html.

10 Donna K. Nagata, Jackie H. J. Kim, and Teresa U. Nguyen, "Processing Cultural Trauma: Intergenerational Effects of the Japanese American Incarceration," *Journal of Social Issues* 71, no. 2 (2015): 356–70.

11 Nagata, Kim, and Nguyen, 363. To this day, many people of Asian descent in the United States are idealized as a model minority while others are exploited as cheap labor or demonized as "a yellow peril." Though far from monolithic, Asian people (from more than twenty origin groups) are lumped together as targets of hate speech and violence. Lately, all Asians groups in the United States have experienced the trauma of rising hate crimes and been blamed for the coronavirus outbreak.

12 For a thorough understanding about transgenerational trauma impacts on Japanese American families, see Donna K. Nagata, Jacqueline H. J. Kim, and Kaidi Wu, "The Japanese American Wartime Incarceration: Examining the Scope of Racial Trauma," *American Psychologist* 74, no. 1 (2019): 36–48.

13 Juana Summers, "Survivors of 1921 Tulsa Race Massacre Share Eyewitness Accounts," interview by Juana Summers, *All Things Considered*, NPR, May 19, 2021, audio, 3:59, https://www.npr.org/2021/05/19/998225207/survivors-of-1921 -tulsa-race-massacre-share-eyewitness-accounts.

14 Les B. Whitbeck et al., "Conceptualizing and Measuring Historical Trauma among American Indian People," *American Journal of Psychology* 3, no. 3–4 (June 2004): 119–30.

15 Isabel Wilkerson, *Caste: The Origins of Our Discontents* (New York: Random House, 2020), 16.

16 One-half to two-thirds of White immigrants to the colonies were brought here under indenture. David W. Galenson, "White Servitude and the Growth of Black Slavery in Colonial America," *Journal of Economic History* 41, no. 1 (March 1981): 39–47, https://doi.org/10.1017/S0022050700042728.

17 Joy DeGruy, *Post Traumatic Slave Syndrome: America's Legacy of Enduring Injury and Healing* (Portland, OR: Joy DeGruy Press, 2017), 118.

18 Alexander L. Hinton, *Annihilating Difference: The Anthropology of Genocide* (Berkeley: University of California Press, 2002), 57.

19 Martin Luther King Jr., *Why We Can't Wait* (New York: Signet Classics, 1963), 146.

20 Mary Annette Pember, "Death by Civilization," *Atlantic*, March 8, 2019, https:// www.theatlantic.com/education/archive/2019/03/traumatic-legacy-indian -boarding-schools/584293/.

21 Pember.

22 Kathleen Brown-Rice, "Examining the Theory of Historical Trauma among Native Americans," *Professional Counselor* 3, no. 3 (December 2013), https:// tpcjournal.nbcc.org/examining-the-theory-of-historical-trauma-among -native-americans/.

23 The National Native American Boarding School Healing Coalition in Minneapolis lists the denominations that ran these schools. They can be found at boardingschoolhealing.org.

24 Brown-Rice, "Historical Trauma," 4–5.

25 R. Yehuda et al., "Low Cortisol and Risk for PTSD in Adult Offspring of Holocaust Survivors," *American Journal of Psychiatry* 157, no. 8 (2000): 1252–59.

26 Martha Henriques, "Can the Legacy of Trauma Be Passed down the Generations?," BBC, March 26, 2019, https://www.bbc.com/future/article/20190326-what-is -epigenetics.

27 Read more about immigration trauma in my book *When Trauma Wounds*.

28 The National Native America Boarding School Healing Coalition's mission is "to lead in the pursuit of understanding and addressing the ongoing trauma created by the U.S. Indian Boarding School policy." "About Us," National Native America Boarding School Healing Coalition, accessed May 19, 2021, https:// boardingschoolhealing.org/about-us/.

Chapter Ten

1 Deborah Cornah, *The Impact of Spirituality upon Mental Health: A Review of the Literature* (London: Mental Health Foundation), 32, https://www.mentalhealth .org.uk/sites/default/files/impact-spirituality.pdf.

2 Robert Grant, *The Way of the Wound: A Spirituality of Trauma and Transformation* (Oakland, CA: Self-published, 1996), 87.

3 McClintock, *When Trauma Wounds*, 133–43.

4 Randy Ellison, personal interview, 2020. See Randy's book about his experience as an adult survivor of clergy sexual abuse: *Boys Don't Tell: Ending the Silence of Abuse* (New York: Morgan James, 2011).

5 Cornah, *Impact of Spirituality*, 32.

6 Ann Weems, *Psalms of Lament* (Louisville, KY: Westminster John Knox, 1995), xxii.

7 Jenkins, "House Chaplain."

8 Julio Cesar Tolentino and Ricardo Bedirian, "Cardiac Autonomic Modulation Related to Prayer May Contribute to the Reduced Cardiovascular Mortality Associated with Religiosity/Spirituality," *Journal of Integrative Cardiology Open Access* 2, no. 2 (July 2019): 1–5, https://doi.org/10.31487/j.JICOA.2019.02.05.

9 Hazem Doufesh et al., "Effect of Muslim Prayer (Salat) on Electroencephalograph and Its Relationship with Autonomic Nervous System Activity," *Journal of Alternative Complementary Medicine* 20, no. 7 (July 2014): 558–62, https://doi .org/10.1089/acm.2013.0426.

Chapter Eleven

1 Manfred Schmitt and Gabriela S. Blum, "State/Trait Interactions," in *Encyclopedia of Personality and Individual Differences*, ed. Virgil Zeigler-Hill and Todd K. Shackelford (Cham, Switzerland: Springer, 2020), https://doi.org/10.1007/978-3 -319-24612-3_1922.

2   Multiple sources report over one hundred sexual assaults each year at military academies, with the numbers rising as protections against retaliation are put in place. Many incidents are never reported.

3   Elijah Megginson, "When I Applied to College, I Didn't Want to 'Sell My Pain,'" *New York Times*, May 9, 2021, https://www.nytimes.com/2021/05/03/health/pets -death-lessons-strength.html?smid=em-share.

4   You can read more about Randy Ellison's journey at boysdonttell.com.

5   DeShazier and Williams, "Movement Gives Back," 31.

6   Frances Hodgson Burnett, *The Secret Garden* (New York: Harper and Row, 1911), 296–97.

ALSO BY KAREN A. McCLINTOCK

*When Trauma Wounds:
Pathways to Healing and Hope*
2019 • Paperback • 180 pages •
9781506434254

HOW TO HEAL FROM TRAUMA AND RESTORE LAUGHTER, LOVE, AND FAITH

When trauma wounds, victims are thrown into unexpected darkness and experience unfamiliar symptoms. Some trauma survivors draw upon a life-long faith in God; others find themselves in a wilderness devoid of spiritual grounding. The recovery stories in this book—including accounts of damaged attached relationships, child sexual abuse trauma, gun violence trauma, and immigration heartbreak—offer diverse pathways to faith and hope.

- Whether you are a trauma survivor, a caregiving pastor or church member, or a friend to a survivor, this book will familiarize you with trauma symptoms and healing strategies.
- If you care for a trauma survivor, McClintock will help you offer victims of trauma the compassion they so badly need.
- If you are a trauma survivor, no matter how long your healing journey might take, it can begin right now.

Available at fortresspress.com and wherever books are sold.